Meet Me in St. Louis

MONDAY
DAILY
MONDAY
OFFICIAL·PROGRAM
WORLD'S·FAIR
LOUISIANA PURCHASE
EXPOSITION
ST. LOUIS, U.S.A.
1904
ST. JOHN

Meet Me in St. Louis

A Trip to the 1904 World's Fair

By Robert Jackson

HarperCollinsPublishers

We would like to acknowledge the following sources for the photographs used in this book: page 2, St. John (World's Fair Program Company), Missouri Historical Society, St. Louis; pages 13, 51, 64 (top), 67, and 79, Official Photographic Company, Missouri Historical Society, St. Louis; pages 26 and 61, Louisiana Purchase Exposition Co., Missouri Historical Society, St. Louis; pages 11, 16, 20, 30, 124, and 130, courtesy of the Library of Congress; pages 32 and 120, courtesy of BoondocksNet.com; page 35, by Emil Boehl, Missouri Historical Society, St. Louis; page 41, by O. E. Laroge, Missouri Historical Society, St. Louis; pages 48, 53, 68, 75, 98, 102, and 103, by Jessie Tarbox Beals, Missouri Historical Society, St. Louis; page 86 (bottom), by Louis Melsheimer, Missouri Historical Society, St. Louis; page 96, by Winfred C. Porter, Missouri Historical Society, St. Louis; pages 126, 127, and 129, courtesy of Max Storm. Map borders and backgrounds throughout courtesy of the Library of Congress. All other photographs from Missouri Historical Society, St. Louis.

Meet Me in St. Louis

Library of Congress Cataloging-in-Publication Data
Jackson, Robert, 1971 Dec. 17–
Meet me in St. Louis : a trip to the 1904 World's Fair / by Robert Jackson.—1st ed.
p. cm.
Summary: Describes the attractions and events that educated, entertained, and mesmerized twenty million visitors at the 1904 St. Louis World's Fair. Includes bibliographical references.
ISBN 0-06-009267-X — ISBN 0-06-009268-8 (lib. bdg.)
1. Louisiana Purchase Exposition (1904 : Saint Louis, Mo.)—Juvenile literature. [1. Louisiana Purchase Exposition (1904 : Saint Louis, Mo.)] I. Title.
T860.B1J33 2004   907'.4778'66—dc21   2003009414

Design by Stephanie Bart-Horvath
1 2 3 4 5 6 7 8 9 10
❖
First Edition

to Rachel

Meet me in St. Louis, Louis,

Meet me at the fair,

Don't tell me the lights are shining

any place but there;

We will dance the Hoochee Koochee,

I will be your tootsie wootsie,

If you will meet me in St. Louis, Louis,

Meet me at the fair.

—chorus from
"Meet Me in St. Louis" (1904)

Contents

CHAPTER 1

A View from the Sky

AFTER A LONG WINTER'S WAIT, the big day arrives. On April 30, 1904, a warm breeze softens the air in St. Louis, Missouri. Tantalizing smells of food swirl around you: hot dogs, barbecue, German sauerkraut, and Louisiana gumbo. Fluffy blue, pink, and white balls of "fairy floss" are everywhere; later this confection will be known as cotton candy. And there's a fizzy new drink called Dr Pepper that, according to its creator, is good for your health.

The spring air is also filled with the sounds and smells of animals, including elephants and giraffes, cattle and sheep. People surround you—more people than you have ever seen in your life, more than you knew were alive on Earth at the same time. They've come from all over St. Louis, from every part of the United States, and from countless countries around the world. Many people are speaking in unfamiliar languages, but you don't need to understand the words to know what

◄ *Reaching 265 feet into the sky, the Ferris wheel became a towering symbol of the grandeur of the 1904 World's Fair.*

everyone is talking about so eagerly. It's Opening Day at the Louisiana Purchase Exposition. The St. Louis World's Fair is about to begin!

You watch the opening ceremony on the Plaza of St. Louis, then hurry west until you approach the fair's most wondrous, awe-inspiring structure: the Ferris wheel. Reaching into the sky like a majestic steel dinosaur, its grand circular shadow stretches far across the fairgrounds. It is taller than any building you have ever seen, taller by far than the lofty brick offices and warehouses along the Mississippi River in downtown St. Louis. As you draw closer, your heart races with fear and excitement; the hulking wheel seems to grow more gigantic with every step you take. You don't even care that there is already a long line or that the ride will cost you the princely sum of fifty cents. When your turn finally comes, you cautiously follow the crowd into a passenger car, which is bigger than a train's caboose.

The giant wheel lurches into motion; you hold your breath and feel yourself moving. How is it possible for such a large car, stuffed to the gills with sixty people, to rise into the air like this? You bravely take a first peek out the windows. Off to the near right, you spot the Abraham Lincoln Exhibit, which houses the actual log cabin where Lincoln lived as a child in Kentucky. Then the rolling gardens and peaceful ponds of the Japanese Pavilion open up in front of you. A bit higher and you can see all of the Jerusalem Exhibit, a miniature version of that Middle Eastern city filled with replicas of ancient buildings. Can this be St. Louis, or have you been transported to a whole new world?

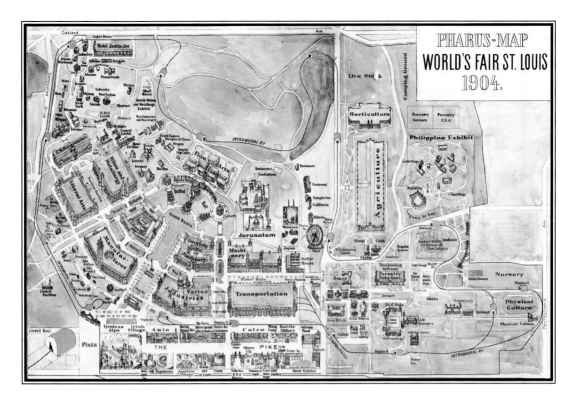

Maps like this one helped visitors find their way around the sprawling, 1275-acre fairground, which had its own railroad system and fire department.

The other passengers gasp with amazement as the car rises, taking you slowly higher, then higher still. People below stroll in the Plaza of St. Louis, and you realize that just a few minutes ago you'd been one single face in that massive crowd. You see the Grand Basin's rippling water and the boats skimming along its surface like toys in a bathtub. The ornate palaces nearby don't look real anymore; they seem more like tiny, intricate models in the distance. Thousands of people in their dark suits and dresses now look like ants as they scuttle in and out of these magnificent buildings.

11

A mile-long strip of rides, games, and shows known as the Pike stretches out like a long, lazy snake far off to your left. The Pike is where a lot of rowdy, rambunctious people can be found anytime of day. Its noise reaches you way up here! Amid the commotion you spot a giant tortoise carrying passengers on its back and a troupe of acrobats building a human tower. You remind yourself to explore the Pike as soon as possible.

When the Ferris wheel brings you to its highest point, you can even see beyond the palaces, beyond the Plateau of States and the far edge of the wooded fairgrounds. In the clear afternoon you can actually make out the distant skyline of downtown St. Louis, more than six miles away. How is it possible for anything but a bird to fly this high? It is as if, for this one thrilling moment, you can see the whole wide world before your very eyes.

After this short pause at its peak, the Ferris wheel gently turns again and you begin to come back down to Earth. You cross to the other side of the car to get a better look at the western view. Beyond the fairgrounds lies an endless landscape of farms and forests; once the Louisiana Territory, this rolling frontier is now part of the United States. To your left you spot the livestock forum and dairy barns that remind you of a county fair. From this distance you can't smell the pigs and cows, but you know they're there. Far ahead you see the enormous Philippine Exhibit. You've heard that entire families from different tribes live inside the imposing walls, presenting a living model of their nation's culture.

Off to the right, beyond Washington University's new sandstone buildings and the wide parade grounds, you see the athletic fields where the Olympic Games will take place later this summer. In the nearby aeronautic fields, some strange men who call themselves scientists attempt to defy gravity in reckless but breathtaking flights into the sky. This sight reminds you of Orville and Wilbur Wright, two brothers who made the first successful airplane flight only several months ago, on December 17, 1903. A bit closer to you stand exotic buildings from nations all over the world, including Brazil and India, France and Great Britain, with their diverse designs and carefully

The Naval Exhibit used miniature ships to present battle scenes for audiences.

Did you forget the time while you stopped to smell the flowers? The enormous floral clock outside the Palace of Agriculture was so big that Ferris wheel passengers could tell the time from several hundred feet in the sky.

planted gardens. Many of them are still under construction, and hundreds of men work hastily in preparation for all the visitors. Winding past them is the Intramural Railroad, a specially built transportation system that takes passengers wherever they want to go on the sprawling fairgrounds. Next to one of the railroad's seventeen stations, the extraordinarily long Palace of Agriculture stretches far to the south. Even from this great height you can see the time on the gigantic floral clock outside its entrance.

As the Ferris wheel brings you slowly back to Earth, you look out over the Life Savings Exhibit Lake, where men demonstrate how they rescue passengers from a sinking ship. The large crowd of spectators applauds enthusiastically at the triumphant conclusion of the scene. Soon the sunken boat will be brought back to the surface and prepared for another performance.

As you gaze out the window, someone nudges you and you start to file out of the car. It feels a bit strange, but also good, to have firm ground under your feet again. As you wander aimlessly through the crowd, your head is still swimming from the great height, the wide blue sky, and the sight of so many wonderful scenes. Your mind races as you try to plan as many adventures as possible for the afternoon. Then you remember that the fair will last not just for this one beautiful spring day, but for seven months—until December 1. That date seems so far away that you might be able to squeeze everything in, if you come often enough. It certainly will be worth a try.

CHAPTER 2

☜ Preparing for the World ☞

ALMOST TWENTY MILLION PEOPLE from around the globe would experience the magnificence of the St. Louis World's Fair. The president of the United States, Theodore Roosevelt, made two visits, once before the fair's opening and again before its close. The great Apache warrior Geronimo spent several months at the fair, signing autographs and posing for pictures with visitors. Scott Joplin, the greatest ragtime composer of his time, wrote and performed a special song called "The Cascades" in honor of the fair.

While these celebrities added a sense of historical majesty, it was the everyday people who made the St. Louis World's Fair the greatest cultural event of its time. A century ago millions of Americans still worked as farmers. It was not uncommon for people to spend their entire lives in rural areas, rarely traveling far from the familiar surroundings of home. Airplanes were nothing more than rickety experiments, and car

☜ *This official French poster encouraged people to make the seven-day journey from Paris to St. Louis for the fair.*

travel was rare. Many people knew little about what was happening in other parts of the world. Of course they couldn't watch the news, because there was no such thing as television. Computers and the Internet were still many decades away from being invented. Not even the radio existed yet! A world's fair was an event that invited everyone to see, hear, and taste the world's culture for the first time.

World's fairs had been popular since London held the first modern and truly international fair in 1851. Known for the beautiful new building where many attractions were housed, it was popularly called the Crystal Palace Exposition. Paris followed with several successful fairs. In 1876 Philadelphia staged the Centennial Exposition, bringing a comparably grand world's fair to America for the hundredth anniversary of the United States.

Then in 1893 the city of Chicago—three hundred miles north of St. Louis—hosted the World's Columbian Exposition. Commemorating the four hundredth anniversary of Columbus's arrival in the New World, this exposition thrilled millions of visitors with its grandeur and set new standards for the size and opulence of a world's fair. Everyone was amazed by the sprawling 633 acres of fairgrounds, huge palaces, strange and exciting entertainments, and the vast crowds that came for six months. St. Louis leaders wanted to show the world that their city could compete with Chicago, its growing rival in everything from business to baseball. They proposed 1903 as the date of their own fair. Its theme, they decided, would be the centennial of the Louisiana Purchase.

The fair was to open on April 30, 1903, one hundred years from the day President Thomas Jefferson completed the Louisiana Purchase. Thirteen states had been formed from the new territory that stretched from the Mississippi River to the Rocky Mountains, and from the Gulf of Mexico to Canada: Arkansas, Colorado, Iowa, Kansas, Louisiana, Minnesota, Montana, Nebraska, North and South Dakota, Oklahoma (which was still known as the Indian Territory in 1904), Wyoming—and Missouri. St. Louis, popularly known as the gateway to the West, was by far the biggest city in this new territory. Its proud citizens wanted the World's Fair to celebrate the Purchase and the people of the West, including Native Americans and pioneer settlers, as well as other cultures from the rest of the world.

In time, the whole city pulled together to make the fair a reality. Thousands of workers contributed to the effort, but one remarkable man played the leading role in bringing the world to St. Louis. His name was David R. Francis. Among the wealthiest businessmen in the city, he was elected mayor of St. Louis while still a young man, and a few years later he became governor of Missouri. Some thought it was only a matter of time before he would become president of the United States. But after serving as governor, he returned to private life as a businessman. An avid admirer of past world's fairs, Francis began drumming up support for the fair in 1896. Four years later he and a small group of St. Louis leaders finally convinced the U.S. Congress to invest five million dollars in the project. These men also secured ten

From its founding in 1764, St. Louis was closely tied to the Mississippi River. The city, shown here in 1859, became a vital connection for the North and South, East and West.

million dollars' worth of state, city, and private investments for the fair. When they formed the Louisiana Purchase Exposition Company to oversee the fair's planning, Francis was named as its president. For the next few years, he would be known around St. Louis simply as President Francis. While planning the fair would be exciting, Francis knew there was a lot of work ahead. His first order of business was transforming St. Louis.

The "Gateway to the West" had many fundamental problems at the turn of the century. Unemployment was high. The quality of drinking water was poor. Heavy smog and air pollution resulted from the use of coal for fuel in homes and the thick dust that swirled up from unpaved streets. Public transportation, including the unreliable streetcar system, seemed to be out of order more often than not, and employees sometimes went on strike to protest their low pay and poor working conditions. Racial and class tensions were accepted as part of everyday life. Blacks were treated with prejudice and disrespect by whites, and clashes were common among ethnic groups as well, including Irish, Italian, and German Americans. In addition to these problems, many city politicians were so greedy and dishonest that most citizens had little trust in local government. Everyone understood that a very small group of wealthy businessmen, known as the "Big Cinch," controlled the city, using their money and connections to maintain power.

This was not the city President Francis wanted the world to see. As a rich businessman and politician, he himself was a central member of the Big Cinch. Yet now that he was organizing the World's Fair, his priorities shifted. President Francis teamed with the new mayor, reformer Rolla Wells, to create what they called a "New St. Louis." They worked to improve water and air quality, increase the efficiency of public transportation, and encourage wealthy citizens to invest in paved streets and other improvements.

In 1901, organizers unanimously approved Forest Park, the big rolling park along the western edge of the city, as the site of the fairgrounds. Eventually, the fairgrounds would include land beyond the park's western and northern borders, covering a total of 1275 acres.

The park would give a home to most of the fair's attractions, from the large palaces to the smaller exhibits. But before the buildings could be started, several problems required attention. The first was that many citizens loved the forest's natural beauty. People often came to play, picnic, and relax on its lush grounds. They did not like the idea of destroying the park for a fair that, however magnificent, would only last for seven months. After receiving many complaints, fair organizers promised not to destroy the whole forest, but this did not satisfy very many people. Sam P. Hyde, a fifty-four-year-old bookkeeper from nearby Belleville, Illinois, frequently visited the park to watch the fairgrounds take shape. He wrote in his diary: "To us it was a sad sight to see the beauties of nature marred, and forest trees that had been fifty years in growing, cut down in an hour."[1]

Another problem was the forest's River Des Peres, a little stream that cut back and forth across the area where many of the fair's largest buildings would stand. River Des Peres often flooded without warning, and its water was polluted by upstream neighborhoods. After discussing the problem, President Francis and the other fair planners decided to

< *Before: Established in 1876 a few miles west of downtown, Forest Park took its name from the thousands of majestic trees that graced its rolling landscape.*

< *After: Despite protesters who did not want Forest Park to lose its natural beauty, organizers cut down many trees in the western half of the park to make way for the fair.*

build a boxed wooden sluiceway underground. Workers spent several months digging a canal thirteen feet deep to house the sluiceway, then covered the new river passage with earth. The sluiceway served as an underground tunnel, allowing the water to pass through the park without threatening fair buildings.

After these alterations had been completed, workers turned their attention to constructing the twelve exhibit palaces. Even though the magnificent palaces required a tremendous amount of planning and work by skilled engineers and laborers, they were not meant to be permanent. They just had to last until the fair closed, after which they'd be torn down.

Once builders completed a palace's wooden interior framework, they covered its exterior with a remarkable substance called "staff." This material was a carefully mixed combination of plaster of paris and fiber, with a tough consistency like that of papier-mâché. Several kinds of fiber were used, including linen, cotton, and even horsehair! While nobody would want a house built of plaster and horsehair, staff proved to be a good material for the palaces. It was so lightweight that workers could hoist large pieces to the tops of buildings with the use of a few ropes, then nail them directly to wooden frameworks. International artists and sculptors could mold staff into any shape they wanted, giving palaces dramatic curves and domes, modeled mostly after classical Greek and Roman architecture. They also created sculptures of people, animals, and imaginary creatures to decorate the palaces and grounds. As the work continued, hundreds of exotic statues sprouted up all over the park. Soon warriors from Greek mythology, powerful buffaloes charging across the western prairie, and heroic Cherokee Indians on horseback dotted the park's landscape, alongside sculptures of Napoleon, Thomas Jefferson, Abraham Lincoln, and other historical figures.

Staff was so lightweight that workers could hoist large pieces with the use of a few ropes. Carpenters appreciated the light material, especially since they were paid only fifty-five cents an hour for their labor.

*Staff sculptures took hundreds of forms in Forest Park,
often re-creating scenes and images from
the American West.*

While the palaces slowly took shape, President Francis realized that the projected Opening Day was coming too quickly. St. Louis had not made all its improvements, and the fairgrounds were far from ready. The fair would have to wait a year. For St. Louisans eager for its arrival, this was a setback, but President Francis turned what might have been a disappointing delay into a great celebration. President Theodore Roosevelt and former President Grover Cleveland both arrived in St. Louis for Dedication Day on April 30, 1903. President Francis welcomed them to explore the unfinished fairgrounds for the next three days and meet the people of St. Louis. Speaking to a crowd of more than fifty thousand citizens, President Roosevelt gave a rousing speech about the importance of the Louisiana Purchase in the growth of the United States. "We meet here today," he said, "to commemorate a great event, an event which marks an era in statesmanship no less than in pioneering."[2] After the ceremony everyone strolled among the half-built palaces, marveling at how much work had been done—and how much still remained.

Another important American who visited St. Louis during the long months of preparation was Mark Twain. The author of many famous novels such as *Adventures of Huckleberry Finn*, Twain had grown up along the Mississippi River before the Civil War. He fondly recalled the energy and excitement he used to find in St. Louis as a young riverboat pilot. With his trademark white hair and white suit, Twain amused St. Louisans and a group of visiting French dignitaries with tall tales of the city's past and predicted the upcoming fair's great success. Sadly, this would be Twain's last visit to St. Louis before his death in 1910.

Curious St. Louisans continued to watch the transformation of their park every week. They came by horse-drawn carriage or streetcar in the evenings and wandered the fairgrounds. Observing the changing scene,

As the palaces began to take shape, curious St. Louisans explored the fairgrounds, imagining what the fair would be like.

they tried to picture what the fair would be like when it finally opened. How would the Palace of Fine Arts look illuminated at night? What would be inside the foreign buildings? How would the fairgrounds feel jammed with thousands of people? So many questions would have to

wait, but everyone could feel the excitement in the air. Until Dedication Day the fair had been just an idea that lived in their imaginations. Now they saw in the changing face of Forest Park that the World's Fair would really take place.

CHAPTER 3

Opening Day at the Main Picture

THOUSANDS OF PEOPLE STREAMED into St. Louis toward the end of April 1904. Opening Day was quickly approaching, and everyone needed a place to stay. Along with Americans from all over the country, travelers came from Caribbean islands, Scandinavian villages, and medieval cities in Spain. Hotels were too expensive for many visitors, so families opened their doors and turned their homes into boardinghouses. They offered extra bedrooms not just to distant relatives, but also to strangers from other states and nations. It was common for an ordinary St. Louis living room to be transformed by gatherings of Brazilian, Russian, and Japanese travelers. Neighborhoods began to feel very different as new faces were seen on the

◄ *A breathtaking morning: April 30, 1904. President Francis greets visitors at the foot of the Louisiana Monument. More than two hundred thousand people converged in Forest Park on Opening Day.*

As this cartoon shows, some residents of St. Louis got tired of having their homes overrun with visiting relatives and friends during the seven months of the fair.

sidewalks, and conversations in languages from French to Chinese were heard in corner stores. Excitement for the fair was growing with the arrival of each new visitor.

Soon after dawn on April 30, in every part of St. Louis, people could feel the energy and anticipation of the day. From the usually quiet, tree-lined neighborhoods to the bustling business district along the river-front, they eagerly headed toward Forest Park. Compact trolley cars rumbled along their steel tracks throughout the buzzing city, delivering passengers to the northern edge of the park. The well-dressed people stepped down and made their way to the high gates at the main entrance of the fairgrounds, where they gladly paid the fifty-cent admission fee. A huge crowd that would swell to two hundred thousand began to assemble for the ceremonies of Opening Day.

From his spot below the Louisiana Monument, President Francis looked with great pride at the sea of bright, hopeful faces filling the Plaza of St. Louis. He could hardly tell where the sprawling crowd ended. Today would be the fulfillment of years of dedication and hard work—from convincing his city to host a world's fair, to planning and overseeing several years of construction in Forest Park. It had not been easy for him, nor for the many laborers who had completed most of the work on the fairgrounds only several days earlier. But their determination ensured the fair's successful beginning. Not even a fierce snowstorm that fell upon the Midwest a week before had slowed them down! Today, with the snow melted, the columns of the palaces sparkled brightly in the sun. Beyond the Louisiana Monument, the Grand Basin stretched far into the distance, its surface reflecting the energy and excitement of the morning. With a note of tremendous hope in his voice, President Francis declared: "Open ye gates! Swing wide ye portals! Enter herein ye sons of men. Learn the lessons taught and gather from it inspiration for still greater accomplishments."[1]

After President Francis's speech, the world-famous bandleader John Philip Sousa and his marching band performed several energetic songs. The crowd grew more enthusiastic with every passing moment. Cheering and clapping along with the music, they stood on tiptoes to get a glimpse of Sousa, whose thick moustache and dark band uniform made him stand out in the sea of people. The mood swelled with the great patriotic march "The Stars and Stripes Forever."

Following the performance, Secretary of War William Howard Taft, later president of the United States, gave a short speech on behalf of President Roosevelt. Then President Francis touched a telegraph key, which sent a message immediately to the White House to let Roosevelt know the fair was ready to begin. From his desk in Washington, Roosevelt responded by touching his telegraph key to officially open the fair. Moments later, when the message arrived back in St. Louis, thousands of colorful flags were raised to their masts and the fountains and waterfalls throughout the fairgrounds began to splash forth. The crowd let out a single great cheer of excitement. The World's Fair had officially begun!

Soon the people dispersed, eager to explore the fairgrounds. From the Plaza of St. Louis they wandered in all directions. Many flocked to the central area of the fair surrounding the Grand Basin, the wide, shallow lake with a network of smaller canals curving around the palaces. This area became known as the Main Picture.

At the Grand Basin visitors could purchase a ride on the small boats and gondolas. The boats skimmed the surface of the lake, carrying young couples seeking a few minutes alone together or excited families gazing at the fair from this terrific viewpoint. A long waterfall called the Cascades splashed down a sweeping hill into the Grand

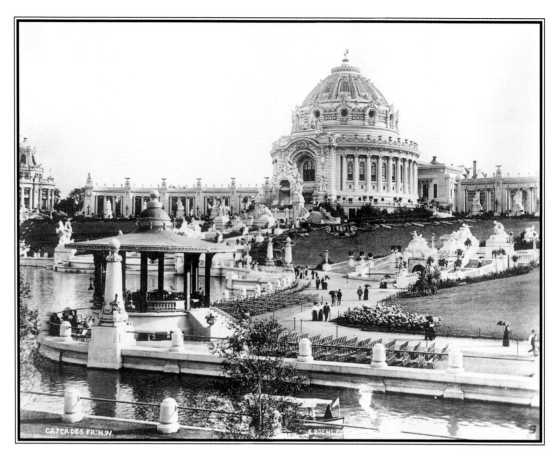

Festival Hall stands majestically above the Grand Basin, presenting one of the most famous images from the fair.

Basin. People climbed the stairs on each side of the Cascades and listened to the peaceful sound of the flowing water.

At the crest of the hill stood Festival Hall, a beautiful domed building set elegantly above the rest of the fairgrounds. Stretching along the sides of Festival Hall was the Colonnade of States, a string of monuments dedicated to each of the thirteen states that had been created from the land in the Louisiana Purchase. Female statues with names

35

From Festival Hall visitors could see the Louisiana Monument rising at the north end of the Grand Basin.

such as Wisdom, Strength, and Courage symbolized the virtues of the American West at the turn of the century.

Inside Festival Hall up to thirty-five hundred visitors could enjoy some of the fair's best music in a spacious auditorium. Classical music boomed forth in earsplitting volume when musicians played the world's largest pipe organ. It was so loud that melodies could often be heard across the Grand Basin in the Plaza of St. Louis! Built in Los Angeles, the organ was so enormous that ten railroad cars were needed to transport it to St. Louis for the fair.

For the rest of the day, visitors strolled in all directions, familiariz-
ing themselves with the strange and wonderful sights of the fair. Then,
after nightfall, President Francis revealed one last Opening Day sur-
prise. From a single location on the fairgrounds, he flipped a switch,
turning on thousands of tiny white lights to illuminate the Main
Picture. Suddenly the majestic palaces took shape in a wondrous city
of light; even the cool evening air felt new and different. White lights
danced like candle flames on the shimmering surface of the water,
reflecting a mirror vision of the night's beauty and peacefulness.
Children and adults alike paused to take in the changed scene with
wide, curious eyes. Electricity was something rarely if ever used, but
on Opening Day it was turned into art for all to see. Inspired by this
sight, Sam P. Hyde later wrote: "Many an hour I sat watching these
lights as one who hates to be awakened from a peaceful dream."[2]
Thousands of others around the fair gazed with wonder and disbelief,
contemplating this enchanting new world that would belong to them
for the next seven months.

CHAPTER 4

☛ Inside the Palaces ☚

EACH DAY VISITORS FLOCKED to the vast palaces around the Grand Basin. Although made of staff, these great buildings stood like ancient marble structures that had been preserved for thousands of years. The most striking thing about them at first was their tremendous size. They were simply massive. Each palace covered several acres of ground and had entrances on all sides. Some even had railroad tracks leading into them! Yet for all their grandeur and architectural beauty, the great number of exhibits was often more impressive. A fairgoer might spend the entire day exploring a single palace without setting foot outside again until closing time. "My idea," said one energetic visitor, "is to take in just as much as I can in the time I have."[1]

PALACE OF MINES AND METALLURGY

Towering fifty-five feet above the other exhibits was a powerful statue of Vulcan, the Roman god of fire, who symbolized the industrial spirit of

◄ *After the fair Vulcan returned to Birmingham, Alabama, where he stands today.*

the Palace of Mines and Metallurgy. This sixty-ton iron giant accompanied the State of Alabama's displays of coal and metal products. Smells of coal, iron, and clay filled the palace air as visitors examined the detailed models of mines and foundries from many states. While the United States was growing to be the world's largest producer of coal, iron, and steel, nations including Japan, Switzerland, and Germany showed the dynamic technology used in mining and metalworking around the globe. Outside, in the nearby Mining Gulch, California, South Dakota, Montana, Illinois, Pennsylvania, and other important mining states built working mines. Led by experts, visitors had the thrilling chance to explore underground caves in search of gold, silver, and other treasures.

PALACE OF VARIED INDUSTRIES

Where could visitors go to watch glassblowers produce beautiful colored bottles, bowls, and vases right before their eyes? In the sprawling Palace of Varied Industries, artisans made furniture, ceramics, and other household objects. Exhibitors displayed thousands of other items—clocks, pottery, and more. The Japanese built an indoor temple in one of the largest exhibits, housing a vast collection of jewelry and sculpture dating from ancient times to the present. Nearby a proud, eight-foot-high iron eagle watched over the German Court of Honor, which displayed hundreds of industrial products, including a wide array of fine watches and an assortment of marble and iron sculpture.

PALACE OF EDUCATION AND SOCIAL ECONOMY

Buzzing with activity every day, the Palace of Education and Social Economy included some of the most popular exhibits at the fair. Students from elementary schools in St. Louis participated in classroom

Lucky St. Louis students were invited to participate in classroom demonstrations at the Palace of Education and Social Economy. Note the boy standing beside the United States map, trying to impress a classmate by showing her the location of St. Louis.

Several Philippine Igorot boys bounce together on the Model Playground's joggling board.

displays, designed to show fair visitors new teaching methods. Instructors taught traditional subjects and everyday household skills—from reading and geography to cooking and sewing. There was even a kindergarten where younger children could play games and listen to music together. The first public American kindergarten had been started in St. Louis in 1873; yet for many international visitors, kindergarten was an innovative concept. They enjoyed watching the children learn and play. For the St. Louis kindergarteners and the other students who participated in exhibits, it was always fun to have such a big audience. It also felt good, of course, to skip school and come to the fair instead.

Visitors were especially impressed by classes for blind and deaf students. They listened in amazement as children as young as four years old expertly played the violin or piano in daily musical recitals. Formal education was not widely available to these students in 1904. However, a blind and deaf Alabama woman named Helen Keller showed what was possible when she graduated from Radcliffe College that year. Following her example, many disabled students would go on to higher education in the twentieth century. The fair's educational exhibits contributed to this progress by giving visitors a new appreciation for all that could be achieved.

MODEL PLAYGROUND

At the nearby Model Playground, children dug in sandboxes and frolicked on swings and slides all day long. Six hundred young gymnasts could even scramble across the monkey bars at once! Lilian Brandt, a woman who visited the playground often, wrote about the unusual "joggling board," which captured everyone's interest. She described this contraption as "a long, flexible plank, each end resting on a crosspiece supported on rockers. The combination of swaying, bouncing, and rocking made possible by the arrangement is something to dream of."[2] While children loved to hang out at the playground, plenty of adults enjoyed spending time there too. Frederick A. Betts of Hartford,

Connecticut, wanted to celebrate his birthday at the playground, so he and his wife arrived with enough cake and ice cream for all sixteen hundred kids who came that day. And on Sunday afternoons, children from all nationalities who lived at the fair came to the Model Playground. Pygmy children from Africa played basketball with Austrian children. Native American kids played soccer with Philippine and Moroccan kids. From many countries and every American state, children made the Model Playground one of the most energetic places on the fairgrounds.

PALACE OF FINE ARTS

Hidden just behind the towering dome of Festival Hall was the Palace of Fine Arts, which displayed a wonderful collection of American art. Huge landscape paintings of the American West gave viewers a sense of the growing majesty of the United States since the Louisiana Purchase. While many countries exhibited works of art in their own national buildings, they also contributed some pieces to the Palace of Fine Arts, making it a required stop for all art lovers.

This priceless collection of art needed a safe home in St. Louis during the fair, a building that would not be in danger of burning down in the event of a fire. So this palace was built of steel, limestone, and brick at a much higher cost than the other palaces. It even had its own network of indoor fire hydrants spaced throughout the galleries, just in case. A visitor might be so busy enjoying a painting that he or she would trip over one of the hydrants without seeing it.

Many companies used the fair as a way to advertise their products, often devising eye-catching presentations like this car-sized teapot.

PALACE OF LIBERAL ARTS

From extremely rare and valuable ancient writings to newfangled, mass-produced typewriters, an entire history of inventions amazed visitors at the Palace of Liberal Arts. Passing through its one-hundred-twenty-foot-high arching entrance, visitors realized that they had entered a world of incredible creations. The steady whirring of machines created a noisy hum, while exhibiting inventors invited curious onlookers to see how their contraptions could be put to practical and daily use. Many decades before the computer printer and copy machine were even dreamed of, visitors watched as bulky, lumbering printing presses cranked out page after identical page. A German exhibit displayed rare maps from hundreds of years ago, as well as examples of the latest developments in photography. Another large exhibit showed off all sorts of ancient Chinese weapons and suits of armor, reminding visitors that cultures around the world had been making unusual and elaborate products for many centuries.

PALACE OF MANUFACTURES

Fashionable models strutted up and down the floor of the Palace of Manufactures wearing long, flowing dresses from France and Italy. A number of Mexican exhibits revealed thousands of different styles of handmade shoes. Tailors and seamstresses from many countries designed and manufactured clothing on the spot, so that visitors could watch the entire process of creation—from raw material to finished product. They could wander into the palace wearing one outfit and emerge only a short while later with new clothes, new shoes, and a brand-new hat! But clothes were not the only items on display. Old and new stoves, furnaces, carpets, and fabrics were also shown throughout the palace. One hardware company decorated its exhibit with hundreds of shiny hammers and saws. In-home heating and ventilation systems, which would come to replace the simple coal stoves used in most homes, gave visitors a glimpse of the future. "It is unthinkable what may all be seen," a young St. Louis lawyer, Edward V. P. Schneiderhahn, wrote in his diary. "The mind reels at the mass of various and wonderful exhibits."[3]

PALACE OF TRANSPORTATION

The Palace of Transportation looked like a train station—a very big train station. Its fifteen acres of exhibit space could hold nine football fields and still have room left over. More than four miles of railway track were used in one exhibit that showed the history of trains from early steam engines to the present. Children could climb inside rickety wooden cabooses and other old train cars from as far back as 1850. Alongside

Visitors loved live demonstrations in the palaces, where they could try out the inventions for themselves.

Before planes were common, inventors experimented with unusual flying machines. Captain T. S. Baldwin's California Arrow *was the most successful airship at the fair.*

these older trains stood many sleek steel railroad cars from countries such as Germany, England, and Ireland. Visitors especially liked to explore the luxurious sleeping cars in these modern trains. With red carpeting and velvet drapes, oak paneling and even private bathrooms, these expensive cars showed how comfortable railroad travel could be.

Boats and strange airships of many shapes and sizes also filled the palace. Many inventors did not expect airplanes to become popular after the Wright brothers' successful flight in 1903, but they still experimented with other kinds of flying machines. Flying contests on the fairgrounds drew huge crowds of spectators. While some were successful, most of the balloonlike contraptions used in these contests were unreliable when they left the ground. Usually they crashed, harmlessly for the most part, minutes after taking off.

In one quiet corner, a few exhibits showed the progress automobiles had made in recent years. But most palace visitors spent their time admiring the powerful locomotives and laughing at the odd airships instead, because cars were not very popular in 1904. Even in large cities like St. Louis, most people rode in horse-drawn carriages or streetcars. Few could have predicted the deep impact that these awkward-looking machines would have in the twentieth century. Just four years later, the Ford Model T would be introduced, and the number of Americans who owned their own automobiles would skyrocket.

PALACE OF ELECTRICITY AND MACHINERY

Hundreds of displays of lights turned the Palace of Electricity and Machinery into a constantly blinking and flashing radiance. Exhibits utilized light for every imaginable purpose. Table and floor lamps revealed alternatives to the candles, kerosene lamps, and gaslights that most people were still using. After all, Thomas Edison had invented the electric lightbulb only twenty-five years earlier, in 1879. Even in 1904 there were so few people who understood the technology of electric lighting that Edison himself came to St. Louis before the fair to help set up all the lights. Electricity was used in many other displays too. For example, some exhibitors demonstrated how X rays, discovered by accident in 1895, could help in the field of medicine.

But perhaps the most popular exhibit was one that invited visitors to talk to each other from one end of the building to the other—on telephones! Long before cellular phones became common and many years before most people had telephones in their homes, visitors gasped in amazement when they heard a friend's voice crackle with static through the small box that served as a phone receiver. Like the lightbulb, the telephone was still fairly new in 1904. Invented by Alexander Graham Bell in 1876 and first exhibited that year at the Philadelphia exposition, the telephone had only recently begun to be used across the United States. It soon would transform American society by connecting people in cities like St. Louis with friends and families in distant cities, small towns, and even farms.

Outside the palace, a wireless telegraph tower reached two hundred fifty feet into the air, nearly as high as the Ferris wheel. It also showed the advancement in long-distance communications by successfully transmitting news stories from the fair to newspaper offices in downtown St. Louis—and once, to the disbelief of many, all the way to Chicago.

PALACE OF MACHINERY

Lights shone everywhere, but they required a lot of energy to keep running. Hidden away in the beautiful Palace of Machinery, an enormous generator worked day and night to provide electric power for

The wonder food of the twentieth century: Puffed rice was first introduced at the fair.

the fair. The generator took up half the floor of the palace and used a total of forty-five thousand horsepower to burn the thousands of lights on the Main Picture, pump water in the Cascades, and keep concessions running smoothly all over the fairgrounds. Most visitors never thought about the source of the fair's electric power until they stood in the same building with the generator. Its overwhelming size and constant, deafening noise made them realize just how much power was being generated for the fair's daily events. The huge machine probably overshadowed some of the smaller but still interesting exhibits at the eastern end of the palace. Metalworking machines and steam engines pumped and hissed, while other machines manufactured all sorts of household goods. The United States had been shifting from an agricultural society to an industrial society during the past few decades, and these machines showed how they too could contribute to mass food production. Machines pumped out barrels and barrels of puffed rice, a brand-new food that millions of Americans would later eat every day. Among the other delicacies being mass-produced were macaroni and a relatively unknown pasty substance called peanut butter. At the fair peanut butter was promoted as a health food for people with bad teeth, but pretty soon people with good teeth were eating it too.

PALACE OF AGRICULTURE

The sweet smell of flowers filled the air outside the Palace of Agriculture, thanks largely to the Floral Clock. Its mammoth face had been made entirely of flowers. The clock's minute hand was seventy-four feet long and moved five feet every minute. Ten people could sit on its long, steel hands without slowing the time for one second!

Inside the twenty-acre palace, which covered more ground than any of the other palaces at the fair, were the farming products of fifteen nations and forty-two U.S. states. Some displays were fairly basic. Rice, tobacco, and cheese stood in huge piles. Heaps of coffee beans from Brazil, Argentina, and Nicaragua added a pungent aroma. But other food was displayed in more creative ways. The State of California's large exhibit included a life-sized elephant made of almonds, and the State of Mississippi unveiled a horse made of pecans. The lofty Missouri Corn Palace, whose high dome resembled the one atop Festival Hall, had been constructed entirely of corn grown in states formed from the Louisiana Purchase. And if anyone had wanted to eat this amazing corn palace, the State of Minnesota supplied more than enough butter—kept in big, refrigerated cases with windows so that visitors could admire it. All this butter was not just sitting there in a big yellow lump: It had been molded into sculptures, which dramatized historical events

Keeping an eye on a man who looks as if he just pocketed a peck of prunes, an almond elephant stood watch over the State of California's enormous display of fruits and vegetables.

Pass the butter, please. . . . An amazing series of refrigerated butter scenes left no doubt about the State of Minnesota's pioneering role in the art of butter sculpture.

as well as everyday scenes from farming life. Edmund Philibert, a young carpenter from St. Louis, described the buttery display in his journal: "There was a house, several cows, a woman milking a cow, a bust of President Roosevelt glasses and all, and several others all very nicely modeled."[4]

Delicious smells of fruit and vegetables—often of extraordinary shapes and sizes—also greeted visitors everywhere they went. Edmund Philibert even reported seeing a potato that "was just about the size and looked like a boxing glove."[5] In another part of the palace, a huge garden of cacti from Texas, New Mexico, and Arizona brought the desert life of the Southwest to the fair. Beyond these prickly giants, an expansive rose garden featured magnificent blooms of red, orange, yellow, and white.

The Missouri Corn Palace gave visitors a majestic, though corny, architectural vision of the plentiful farmland west of the Mississippi.

PALACE OF HORTICULTURE

More varieties of plants were displayed in the nearby Palace of Horticulture, which also hosted livestock exhibits and many events reminiscent of traditional country fairs. Fairgoers from rural communities especially enjoyed learning about new farming and breeding products and methods. They were also entertained by horse and poultry shows, cattle auctions, milking competitions, and a rare, thrilling visit by a famous cow named Juliana de Kol. Why was Juliana so famous? She held a number of world records for producing the most milk of any bovine in history! Juliana's private railroad car—draped in California's state colors of green and orange—arrived early one morning at the train station. Hundreds of fans waited to greet her, and they let out such a cheer when she disembarked that the famous cow became frightened and tried to run away. Luckily her lifelong attendant was able to calm her down and lead Juliana to her private "suite" in the livestock barns, where visitors flocked all summer to check out her world-famous udders.

PALACE OF FORESTRY, FISH AND GAME

Just north of the Floral Clock stood the Palace of Forestry, Fish and Game, which delighted visitors with scenes from nature in the American West. Photo exhibits showed how settlement was changing the West; these images helped create awareness of the need to preserve America's wild spaces—a measure President Roosevelt had been advocating.

There were also large aquariums holding thousands of fish—trout, whitefish, blue pike, perch, and other species. Unfortunately, exhibitors had not sufficiently prepared some of the tanks for such variety. Great numbers of fish died because of polluted water. Everyone was amazed to find that several thousand minnows from Lake Erie did not seem to mind the pollution. They just kept on swimming. Later in the summer, many more fish died because the water in some tanks was too warm. Finally, by late August, new refrigerated tanks solved that problem, giving the fish a safe, comfortable place to swim.

EXPLORING THE PALACES

The sheer exhaustion a visitor felt after exploring just one of the palaces quickly became a concern. Bulletins urged everyone to wear comfortable shoes, take plenty of rest breaks, and drink lots of water. One story described the familiar sight of a man who had tried to see as much as possible in one day at the fair:

"By George," said a robust farmer, as he fell into a seat in the plaza about five o'clock one afternoon, "I've plowed all day many a time; and I know hard work as well as the next man. But this is the hardest day's work I've ever done—it uses you up." But he had no sooner laid his feet out in a comfortable position than he began to talk with enthusiasm about what he had seen. "It uses you up, but it's worth it."[6]

CHAPTER 5

⟡ Wide World of Architecture ⟡

T HE LATE SPRING GRADUALLY WARMED into summer, and everyone grew more and more familiar with the seemingly endless fairgrounds. The park became a comfortable world all its own. Passing on wide walkways between the stately palaces, visitors found yet another world in the southeast corner of the fairgrounds. This tree-lined part of Forest Park with gentle, rolling hills was known as the Plateau of States.

Thirty-eight states and four territories—Alaska, Arizona, Oklahoma, and New Mexico—had buildings on the fairgrounds. Among existing states, only Alabama, Colorado, Nebraska, North Carolina, North Dakota, and Wyoming were not able to construct their own buildings, although they presented exhibits in palaces or other areas of the fair. State buildings quickly became gathering spots for visitors from home, wherever home might be. People who traveled to the fair from distant places like California and Alaska were especially delighted to find common places to meet.

◄ *A group of authentic totem poles stood watch in front of Alaska's exhibit.*

Each building was designed to reflect its state's character and history. Many New England states were proud of their role in the settling and founding of our nation and displayed historical furnishings in beautiful colonial buildings. Connecticut's elegant mansion was filled with valuable antiques—including a chair brought aboard the *Mayflower* by the Pilgrims, a Chippendale writing desk from 1765, and George Washington's chair from the First Continental Congress.

New states and territories in the Northwest celebrated their natural bounty. The State of Washington, an important center of the timber industry, designed a towering "wigwam" structure with heavy wooden planks made from its evergreen forests. Inside, a hand-operated elevator lifted visitors nine stories to give them a stunning view of the fairgrounds. The territory of Alaska, not admitted as a state until 1959, built one modern building on-site with its forests' timber. Two smaller buildings were brought to St. Louis all the way from the remote town of Sitka. Rows of towering totem poles, carved with the faces of birds, beasts, and mythical creatures, surrounded these buildings. Inside, plants, furs, and a beautiful collection of photographs revealed Alaska's natural scenery. Alaskan families from several indigenous groups spent the entire fair in St. Louis, making crafts and telling stories that left visitors with a deep impression of life in the far Northwest.

Many southern states designed replicas of antebellum plantation homes—stately mansions with low, wide porches framed by rows of classical white columns. The State of Virginia built a smaller version of Monticello, the country estate of former President Thomas Jefferson. In the same spirit, the State of Tennessee constructed a reproduction of the Hermitage, the famous home that former President Andrew Jackson had built for his family near Nashville. Inside the lovely colonial-style building, President Jackson's personal belongings, including his clothing, books, and guns, made it

One of the most popular fair destinations was this log cabin, where young Abraham Lincoln had lived in Hardin County, Kentucky. The cabin had been transported to St. Louis in pieces and reassembled on the fairgrounds.

The Texas State Building was one of the largest and most unusual of those at the fair. It was shaped like an enormous five-point star to remind everyone of Texas's nickname: the Lone Star State. Visiting Texans took great pride in the building's size and originality.

feel like the war hero and president from seventy years earlier was visiting the fair just like everybody else.

Another popular building was the State of Louisiana's historic replica of the New Orleans Cabildo, the Spanish government headquarters where the Louisiana Purchase had been finalized in 1803. With its curved, arching columns and ornate iron grillwork, the building looked as if it had been lifted straight from its home on Chartres Street. Viewing Napoleon's china cabinet and the small wooden desk on which American and French officials had signed the treaty, visitors imagined what this historical moment might have been like.

The biggest state building—and one of the most expensive—was built by the State of Missouri. More than three hundred feet long, it looked like a slightly smaller version of the palaces around the Grand Basin. The building featured a huge gold dome that rose from its high roof. An indoor auditorium had space for one thousand visitors to enjoy lectures, concerts, and banquets. The governor and other state politicians even had private offices here, which they used when they weren't walking through the fairgrounds, welcoming visitors.

The Missouri State Building quickly became a great favorite. For more than six months, visitors enjoyed its beauty and majesty, but then disaster struck. On the night of November 19, less than two weeks before the close of the fair, an uncontrollable fire consumed the building. There had been several smaller fires in other highly flammable buildings over the summer, but none as big or as dangerous as this one.

Visitors huddled at a safe distance and watched in tears as the magnificent building went up in flames. Courageous firefighters from the park's own fire department struggled in vain to fight the enormous blaze, which spread quickly from an unknown source within the building. As the roof began to collapse in several spots and the fire pushed its way to the outer walls of the building, hundreds of pieces of furniture—some of them historic and very valuable—were destroyed. The firefighters quickly saw that they could not stop the fierce blaze, but

Sitting atop a hill near the U.S. Government Building, the Missouri State Building majestically overlooked the Plateau of States.

The building's blackened remains show the devastating effects of the November 19 fire.

they did their best to keep it from spreading. Through a huge hole in the roof, a single American flag floated high above the dark smoke over the center of the fire—more than a hundred feet off the ground. Onlookers stared in disbelief as the flag wafted beyond the burning walls and drifted gently down to the ground, unharmed.

The next morning people rushed to see if the raging fire had spared anything in the building. A few chunks of the outer walls were still standing, along with several columns. As for the interior, a few wooden chairs had somehow avoided destruction; later, they found a new home in the Missouri governor's mansion in Jefferson City. Everything else was ruined. The beautiful building had symbolized Missouri's proud traditions and strong presence at the fair, and the sight of the majestic building's burned ruins was crushing. For the remaining days of the fair, visitors came and sat at the foot of the hill where the building had stood. The unfortunate demise of the Missouri State Building reminded them that no matter how beautiful and exciting the fair was, it too would come to an end all too soon.

U.S. GOVERNMENT BUILDING

Just down the hill from the Missouri State Building stood another magnificent structure: the United States Government Building. The U.S. government had participated in expositions before 1904, but this eight-hundred-foot-long building was the largest such structure ever built for a world's fair. It contained a history museum, a sizable U.S.

Post Office Department exhibit, and half of an American battleship, complete with cannons and other weapons. Each government department, from Congress to the Supreme Court, had its own exhibit, where visitors learned about the American political system and met the many government officials who spent time in St. Louis during the fair.

FOREIGN BUILDINGS

Along the western edge of Forest Park, many foreign countries had designed and constructed their own buildings. Often these included beautiful museums, gardens, and restaurants, giving visitors who might never travel abroad a rare look at different cultures. Many people from these nations came to St. Louis, first to help build the structures and then to become a living, breathing part of their countries' exhibits.

Like the state buildings, foreign buildings and their exhibits usually taught important parts of their countries' history. Germany built a replica of its Palace of Charlottenburg—a striking eighteenth-century castle with historical scenes depicted on its walls. Art and artifacts from German museums were displayed inside. France constructed a reproduction of the stately Grand Trianon at Versailles. The palace housed tapestries, furniture, porcelain, wood carvings, and elaborate painted murals tracing the history of France from medieval times through the French Revolution of 1789–95. Near the new campus of Washington University, Great Britain built a replica of the Orangery at Kensington Palace. The long, elegant gardens provided the feeling of an old English

An impressive replica of the Palace of Charlottenburg served as the home for Germany's wide array of exhibits, from military artifacts to works of art.

nature preserve, orderly and peaceful. Inside, one popular exhibit showed a great collection of swords, shields, and suits of armor. Belguim's striking building was between the smaller Cuban and Italian buildings. It was shaped like a small train station with a curved roof; gorgeous landscape murals covered its outer walls. Exhibits of steel and iron products vividly reminded visitors that this small European country was an important force in modern business and industry.

Most Americans knew little about Europe in 1904, but they knew even less about Asia. Mysterious tales and superstitions about Asian cultures were quite common, so visitors approached these displays with great interest. China's buildings were traditional, with bamboo and teakwood covering the exteriors in Mandarin style. But it was

President Francis welcomed Prince Pu Lun and other Chinese officials to St. Louis for Opening Day. The prince would become a familiar sight on the fairgrounds in 1904, exploring many exhibits.

Prince Pu Lun who made the deepest impression upon visitors. The prince arrived in St. Louis for Opening Day, accompanied by a large group of servants and other Chinese officials. Quickly adopting the adventuresome spirit of the fair, he explored the grounds on foot. Visitors could not quite believe that the young man before their very eyes was indeed a prince from China. One of the most distinguished foreign dignitaries at the fair, Prince Pu Lun spent the rest of his time in St. Louis as an honored guest of President Francis and other St. Louis leaders.

Standing a few blocks south of China's buildings, the Japanese Pavilion formed a particularly unusual collection of buildings, gardens, and lakes. Japan was at war with Russia in 1904, but despite such difficult circumstances at home, its leaders insisted on representing their nation at the fair. Their exhibit showed the world that this ancient nation isolated in the Far East was also a modern country with great industrial potential. Daily events included concerts by Japanese musicians and traditional tea ceremonies in the Enchanted Garden. Nearby exhibits emphasized Japan's technological achievements in areas such as shipbuilding, manufacturing, railroads, and textiles.

Japan's Enchanted Garden invited visitors to escape from the fair's hurried pace and experience the tranquility of traditional tea ceremonies and daily performances by Japanese musicians.

Japanese men and women showed visitors the whole process of making one of their nation's major products—silk. From nurseries of silkworm cocoons to displays of beautiful kimonos, scarves, and fans, silk production was illustrated in step-by-step detail.

India, Ceylon, and Siam offered different perspectives on cultures of the East, and many other nations from around the world contributed to the fair in unique ways. The North African country of Morocco presented its culture with impressive buildings and exhibits, as did Argentina, Guatemala, Mexico, and Puerto Rico. Many countries operated restaurants inside or near their buildings, and smells of exotic foods became common throughout the fairgrounds: falafel and baba ghanoush from the Middle East, paella from Spain, sushi from Japan, and many, many others. The Latin American country of Nicaragua created its own little world within the fair. While the building itself was quite simple, officials had transplanted all sorts of trees and plants from Nicaragua. Visitors who wandered onto the grounds found themselves transported into a lush forest of unfamiliar tropical vegetation. More than two hundred specimens of medicinal roots and flowers, and many different kinds of coffee, were displayed inside the building.

Still other nations did not build their own structures at the fair but exhibited aspects of their cultures in some of the large palaces. European countries including Bulgaria, Denmark, Hungary, Monaco, Portugal, and Russia presented such exhibits. And of course, hundreds of countries were represented by the spirit of their peoples. A number of Middle Eastern and African natives arrived in St. Louis from Egypt, Ethiopia, Persia, and Turkey. From the South Pacific, groups came from as far away as Australia and New Zealand. And from South and Central America and the Caribbean, diverse peoples came from countries including Colombia, Costa Rica, Haiti, Honduras, Paraguay, Peru, and Venezuela.

This international presence helped the exposition to become a world's fair in the truest sense and educated millions of visitors by giving them personal experiences of so many diverse cultures and ways of life. Reporter Walter H. Page described these fairgoers: "Everybody who comes here—country-folk and all—has an intelligent interest in the foreign exhibits, in the foreign buildings, in facts about the life, the work, and the arts of other peoples."[1]

By drawing so many nationalities to St. Louis at one time, the fair created a great deal of cultural activity in the city. Even after most of these people had returned to their homelands, St. Louis would continue to feel the mark they had left, and its interest in global cultures would remain strong. And of course, many foreign visitors returned home with new impressions and ideas about the unusual people who lived in the United States.

CHAPTER **6**

Illusions on the Pike

MORE THAN SIX THOUSAND PERFORMERS from around the world came to entertain on the Pike's "mile of marvels." Plays, concerts, circus tricks—more than forty different shows were staged in all, some in theaters and others right in the center of the wide walkway. Fifteen hundred animals, from zebras to polar bears, lived on the Pike during the fair, and many of them were entertaining performers too.

Without a doubt, the Pike was the loudest area on the fairgrounds. Dozens of men called "spielers" or "barkers" shouted into megaphones for hours, trying to attract people to rides and shows. Many of the rowdiest fairgoers ended up at the Pike, turning out in huge droves every morning and staying long after the palaces closed each night. Their noise was almost deafening. Sam P. Hyde visited the Pike on Thanksgiving Day and described the boisterous scene in detail: "Trouble had begun early on the Pike," he wrote. "A thousand

73

◁ *Laughter coming from the maze of mirrors and the circular slide inside the Temple of Mirth could be heard all the way out on the Pike.*

pedestrians thronged the great thoroughfare beneath ten thousand electric lights, whilst the din of cow bells, whistles, megaphones, the infernal yelling of barkers mingled with the boom of cannon in the sham battle shows, and every body making all the noise they could with every conceivable device . . . rendered a pandaemonium that I don't expect to hear again this side of Hades."[1]

Tyrolean Alps and an Irish Village

A towering, sweeping mountain range greeted visitors on the eastern end of the strip. Molded out of staff and painted to appear snowcovered, it formed the backdrop to the Tyrolean Alps—a group of German shops and a restaurant with enough space for more than a thousand customers. Many adults relaxed in the spacious beer garden, escaping the commotion of the Pike while sipping the world's best beers.

Ireland chose to set its exhibit along the Pike, where it added to the enthusiastic, festive mood. Inside its gates the Irish Village featured a number of buildings modeled on well-known landmarks, including the Irish House of Parliament, St. Lawrence's Gate at Drogheda, and Blarney Castle. There was a museum of Irish history, art, and industry—as well as a theater where Celtic music and dance were performed several times a day. The actors and musicians had all come from Ireland. Exhibitors tried to represent the Irish country and culture as authentically as possible. Even the soil used in the village had been imported from Ireland!

The Tyrolean Alps gave visitors a chance to eat, drink, and imagine themselves in the middle of the mountains in Europe. There was even an electric tram that took passengers on a winding trip through the mountains.

A fair publication advertised the sights of Under and Over the Sea.

ILLUSIONS

Long before computers popularized virtual reality, the Pike offered virtual tours called illusions. One of the most popular was named Under and Over the Sea. Here visitors boarded an actual submarine that could hold up to two hundred fifty people at once. After the doors closed securely, the ship descended into a large tank of water, as if plunging deep beneath the ocean's surface. Through large portholes passengers watched the undersea life: fish swam past the windows, aquatic plants swayed gently back and forth, and sunken pirate ships rested silently on the ocean floor. The submarine cruised peacefully through the water as though traveling up the Seine River to Paris. Finally it surfaced. Passengers disembarked onto a small platform, where they boarded an elevator and rode to the top of the Eiffel Tower for a grand view of Paris at night. The City of Lights looked like a constellation of thousands of tiny stars shining brightly from below. But this "city" was actually a giant model—constructed one building at a time from twenty-five thousand pieces of cardboard and nearly as many white lights. While everyone knew it was just an illusion, they still gazed in wonder at the scene's brilliance and beauty. Lastly passengers climbed aboard a long, balloonlike airship. They flew across the Atlantic Ocean and looked upon New York City before finally settling down again at the St. Louis World's Fair.

Another illusion named Hale's Tours and Scenes of the World offered a different kind of journey. A "conductor" stamped train tickets and directed passengers into a room that looked like a railroad car.

The car rocked and swayed while travelers watched scenic landscapes rush by. They were actually seeing a film that had been shot from the window of a moving train! Since the movie industry was still in its infancy in 1904, these images were the first motion pictures that most visitors had ever seen. Few could have guessed that movies would become such a huge part of life in the twentieth century.

AMUSEMENT PARK RIDES

In a time when people rarely rode on trains, the most popular ride on the Pike was the Scenic Railway. During a thrilling trip that mixed roller-coaster action with illusions, a small, open-air railway car shot passengers up and down steep hills at breakneck speed. Fairgoers at the other end of the Pike could often hear the delighted—and terrified— screams of the riders as they sped past panoramic scenes of cities and meadows, over rushing rivers, and down into dark underground caves. All of these sights of "nature" were, of course, models and large painted murals constructed just for the ride.

Much noise and excitement also came from Shoot the Chutes—a wide, steep slide that sent carloads of screaming thrill-seekers racing into a deep pool of water. Sam P. Hyde described in his diary his own moment of terror: "I paid my dime and ascended to the dizzy platform. A number of young people crowded into the car and the signal was given. 'Now yell as loud as you can' said I, 'for that is part of the fun.' . . . And they yelled all right. I will not attempt to describe the sensation, but no native born American will shoot the chutes and not yell. We struck the water and shot into the air again and then were towed to the landing. I did not notice till I got out that I had lost my glasses in the shock. Returning I fished in the water and dirt in the bottom of the boat till I found them. I did not care to shoot again but I have been glad ever since that I did."[2]

From the looks on their faces, you'd think these children had just learned there was no more ice cream at the fair—or perhaps they had wanted to ride a camel along the Pike instead.

Fairgoers and animals mingled peacefully at Hagenbeck's Zoological Paradise.

Hagenbeck's Zoological Paradise & Animal Circus

Children and adults came face-to-face with many of Carl Hagenbeck's creatures—big and small—from around the world. One advertisement described the scene as "an immense open air panorama in which wild and domesticated animals roam at large without so much as a mosquito netting between them and the spectators." Families played with the many domesticated animals and small birds—and the animals didn't seem to mind at all. There was, however, a nearly invisible fence separating this safe area from "the African Plains," where wild elephants, lions, tigers, zebras, and giraffes milled around together. And in the far distance, the land sloped upward into high peaks. Mountain goats and polar bears climbed and played in what looked like a white world of ice and snow—another creation of staff and paint, built by workmen for the fair.

In his own three-thousand-seat theater, Hagenbeck presented daily circus performances with trained animals—from seals and birds to lions and tigers. Sometimes he even invited children from the audience to help with the acts. Meanwhile, outside on the Pike's walkway, children rode camels, elephants, llamas, ostriches, and giant tortoises. Fairgoers would often see two different acts overlapping each other's space. In one hilarious case, two children rode a giant tortoise—right through the middle of a troupe of daredevil Japanese acrobats! The stunned acrobats were furious that their act had been interrupted, but the large crowd approved with cheers and laughter. The tortoise just kept rambling along as slowly as before, totally unaware of the commotion it had created.

JIM KEY

Another animal novelty along the Pike was Jim Key, the Educated Horse. Hailed by his owner as "a horse with a human brain," Jim amazed crowds with marvelous feats in mathematics and reading. He counted money, told the time of day, and even used the telephone! Edmund Philibert witnessed Jim's performance and described it in his diary: "He spelled, Hires Root Beer, trust, and several other words by picking up lettered blocks with his teeth. . . . Some one asked, How much is 3 x 6 + 5 - 9? and Jim picked out the block numbered 14. After the performance we went to see the stable. The man in charge said it took six years to train Jim and, he is being taught new tricks every day."[3] Jim Key was valued at the extraordinary figure of one hundred thousand dollars. A true celebrity like Juliana de Kol, he even traveled in his own private railroad car.

WILD WEST, INDIAN CONGRESS AND ROUGH RIDERS OF THE WORLD

Fifty-one different tribes of Native Americans came together at the Wild West, Indian Congress and Rough Riders of the World exhibit. Since they had come from many regions throughout North America, a good many of these Native American peoples were meeting one another for the first time. Curious onlookers watched as Navajos wove blankets, Moquis made pottery, and various other tribes performed complex ceremonies including the sun dance, snake dance, and a

Legendary Apache warrior Geronimo became one of the Pike's greatest attractions. He lived at the fair for four months in 1904 before returning to his reservation in Oklahoma.

terrifying scalp dance. Visitors also explored the tipis and wigwams built on the fairgrounds. And, of course, everyone enjoyed meeting Geronimo, the seventy-five-year-old legendary Apache warrior. He signed autographs for ten cents each; depending on his mood, the price for his photograph ranged between fifty cents and two dollars. Geronimo would even sell his hat for the wildly expensive price of five dollars—then coolly pull a new one from under the table, place it on his head, and wait for another buyer.

In an open-air arena next to the Native American assembly, cowboys from Texas, Oklahoma, Colorado, New Mexico, and California demonstrated their great skill in rifle shooting, steer roping, and six-horse chariot races. Miss Lucille Mulhall—champion lady rider of the world—thrilled crowds with her skill in handling and tying Mexican steers. Also performing were Will Rogers and Tom Mix, who would later become two of the greatest stars of the early cinema. Rogers and Mix were among the hundreds of real-life cowboys who dramatically portrayed scenes from the legendary Old West. Visitors loved these performances just as much as they would love those western movies. They cheered as courageous Pony Express riders delivered mail through hostile Indian territory, fighting off attacks at every turn. Custer's Last Stand from the 1876 Battle of the Little Bighorn was also a thrilling and gruesome spectacle for visitors. It was ironic that Rogers, a native of Oklahoma and one-quarter Cherokee Indian, should perform as the last U.S. cavalry soldier killed at Custer's Last Stand.

In other performances bands of Indians on horseback attacked stagecoaches and battled American soldiers in improvised scenes. Fairgoers didn't seem bothered that these fierce and bloodthirsty Indians were unlike the people who made up the nearby Native American assembly. They had come for an exciting show about the mythical Old West and didn't care that the scenes being performed were largely historically inaccurate.

Hales Fire Fighting Exhibition

Other popular heroes of the day were celebrated at the Hales Fire Fighting Exhibition. Its museum held a large collection of the rarest and most unusual firefighting equipment in the world. One display on the history of firefighting included everything from a horse-drawn pump that a young George Washington had once used to the latest design in fire engines. The New York Volunteer Firemen's Association also showcased its own large collection of equipment, alongside displays from many other American cities.

The most exciting part of the exhibit took place in the theater, where a group of firemen dramatized their work in a one-hour performance. Before a nervous audience, the firemen climbed out of bed at the fire station, jumped into their gear, and slid down poles to reach their horse-drawn fire engines. Then they rushed to an enflamed six-story building, where actors screamed for help from the burning windows. With aerial hooks and long ladders they rescued everyone in a tense spectacle. The firemen battled the fire and quenched it, to the great relief of the crowd. Afterward, the building collapsed into a huge pile of rubble, only to be constructed again for the next show. (Amazingly, no actual fire was used in this performance; the illusion of a burning building was created with steam, stained glass, smoke, and lights!) At the conclusion of the performance, a group of boy firefighters—ages ten to twelve—marched onstage in tight formation, carrying their own small hooks and hoses. They even had their own miniature fire engine and pump drawn by a

Nobody knows just how many ice-cream cones were eaten at the fair, but these visitors happily counted themselves among the satisfied customers.

team of Shetland ponies. The audience always loved this part of the show and cheered these future firefighters with great delight.

POPULAR TREATS AND TALES

According to a popular tale, it was a hot summer day on the Pike when a teenage ice-cream vendor named Arnold Fornachou ran out of serving dishes. A young immigrant from Syria named Ernest Hamwi, who sold thin waffles called zalabias at a nearby booth, saved the day. He rolled one of his waffles into the first ice-cream cone the world had ever seen, spontaneously creating a new craze. Thousands and thousands of ice-cream cones were eaten in St. Louis that summer, making them the most popular treat at the fair.

Some people also claim that the hot dog made its first appearance on the Pike. Nobody knows who introduced this tubular delicacy to St. Louis, but the hot dog was a smash hit with hungry fairgoers from around the world. Iced tea also enjoyed a strong reception at the fair. Since summer days were so hot in St. Louis, people dumped chunks of ice into hot tea to cool it, creating a classic American beverage.

Most likely the ice-cream cone, hot dog, and iced tea existed for several years before 1904. But they certainly became much more popular as millions of people enjoyed them for the first time at the fair.

≺ *Opposite, bottom: A contortionist twists like a pretzel in one of many acrobatic acts performed on the Pike.*

CHAPTER 7

☞ The Great Wheel ☜

FTER THE EIFFEL TOWER MADE its spectacular premiere at the
Paris Universal Exposition of 1889, a Pittsburgh bridge builder
named George W. Ferris thought America needed a similarly majestic
structure. So he set out to create one. Ferris decided to design a large,
revolving wheel instead of a single tall tower. His magnificent wheel
debuted in Chicago at the 1893 World's Columbian Exposition,
where it became a very popular and profitable success.

Ferris was not the first person to think of the revolving wheel, but
he used his knowledge of modern engineering to create one that was
far bigger and stronger than any the world had ever seen. After
Chicago's fair, the wheel had been dismantled and stored in a ware-
house. Nobody could find a permanent home for something so huge.
But, in 1904, the wheel made a grand reappearance in St. Louis.

◁ *Hundreds of workers helped to assemble the Ferris wheel after its arrival
from Chicago. It was an enormous project, with 175 railroad cars needed to
transport the wheel's parts to St. Louis along the western edge of Forest Park.*

The Ferris wheel's axle weighed 70 tons, making it the single heaviest part of the 4,200-ton wheel.

The thick central axle, which was the largest single piece of steel ever forged, stretched to a length of forty-five feet. Two massive steel towers supported the axle one hundred forty feet above the ground. Hundreds of workers were needed to put all the pieces together. A pair of one-thousand-horsepower reversible engines powered the wheel, enabling it to turn in both directions. Like the rest of its features, the wheel's passenger cars were enormous. Each of the thirty-six cars was the size of a large school bus and had room for sixty people. The entire wheel could carry 2,160 people at the same time!

Once assembled, the wheel stood an astounding 265 feet high. Much taller than the fair's palaces and more than twice as high as the tallest buildings in downtown St. Louis, it loomed over the park like a huge mutant bicycle wheel. Fairgoers gazed in wonder at the great wheel from below, and their hearts raced as the wheel lifted them far above the fairgrounds for the view of a lifetime.

Beginning on Opening Day, large crowds gladly paid fifty cents for a ride on what was officially named the Observation Wheel but was known more commonly as the Ferris wheel. Considering that lunch at the fair cost about a dime, a fifty-cent Ferris wheel ride was an expensive proposition. But to more than three million visitors, it was a small price for such a rare experience. On August 20, after enjoying the wheel with a companion, satisfied customer Edmund Philibert wrote in his diary: "May did not want to go on it at first; she was afraid she would get dizzy, but afterwards she was glad. . . . The view from the top of the wheel was very fine. We made two trips in the afternoon, and in the evening two more to view the illumination which looked fine."[1]

Fairgoers didn't just ride on the Ferris wheel. Wealthy people organized lavish banquets inside the cars. With servants and cooks in attendance, they could dine comfortably while enjoying the view. One young couple decided to get married on the Ferris wheel. They actually rode into their car at the beginning of the ceremony on two ponies. It was also reported that a "woman daredevil" named Maude Nichols stood on top of a car and rode around twice—accompanied by her husband and a fair official!

Even Geronimo took a break from his usual spot at the Wild West exhibit for a ride on the wheel. Accompanying the Apache warrior were several American soldiers who guarded him at all times, since he was still officially considered a prisoner of war. "One time the guards took me into a little house that had four windows," Geronimo later said. "The little house started to move along the ground. I was scared, for our house had gone high up in the air, and the people down in the Fair Grounds looked no larger than ants. I had never been so high in the air, and I tried to look out into the sky. Then they said, 'Get out!', and when I looked we were on the street again. After we were safe on the land I watched many of these little houses going up and coming down, but I cannot understand how they travel. They are curious little houses."[2]

Toward the end of the fair, President Francis and other organizers pondered this question: What could be done with the wheel? Dismantling the giant structure would be expensive, and transporting the steel beams and passenger cars would cost even more. Besides, where would the wheel go? Nobody had a practical solution, and it soon became clear that St. Louis was the last stop for this Ferris wheel.

And so, many months after the fair ended and the wheel's cars had been removed and sold, the towering structure came crashing down to earth. With a single blast of dynamite, workers reduced the elegant steel circle—symbol of the fair's monumental size and hopeful spirit—into a tangled heap of scrap metal. "It was like watching the execution of an old friend," noted Arthur Proetz, a Washington University student who witnessed the event. "When the dynamite went off under its base, the world seemed to stand still for a tragic moment as it shuddered, crumpled, and sank slowly to the earth."[3] People were free to haul away what they could carry from the pile of rubble. According to legend the rest of the great wheel—including the giant central axle—was buried in Forest Park. Many felt it was a sad ending for such a triumph of design and engineering, and fairgoers remembered the wheel with awe and affection. Sam P. Hyde summed up the feelings of millions of visitors with a single sentence: "It was the only one of its kind and truly wonderful."[4]

The remains of the Ferris wheel lay in a heap of twisted metal after the fair.

CHAPTER 8

☞ Faces of the Fair ☞

SUMMERTIME ALWAYS BROUGHT hot, humid days to St. Louis, but in 1904 it also brought people—millions and millions of them. Wanting the fair to rival Chicago's exposition, President Francis had spent a great deal of time and money on publicity. Before the fair began, he traveled to Europe to recruit exhibitors and lure fairgoers. Other fair organizers also ventured around the world to promote the event. Drawn by all sorts of advertisements—in newspapers and magazines, on billboards across the country, and from the stories of friends and family—people came to St. Louis. They flooded the Plaza of St. Louis each morning when the fair opened. They lounged on long benches along the Plateau of States. They examined the palace exhibits and then bought ice cream from the fair's fifty different ice-cream stands. Many relaxed in large wicker "wheelchairs" while college students pushed

≺ *Fairgoers who got tired of walking the endless fairgrounds could rent a roller chair and driver. Many college students from around the country worked as drivers, often becoming tour guides as well.*

Long before radio and television, billboards advertised the fair throughout the United States. This billboard was posted in Minneapolis, Minnesota.

them wherever they wanted to go. Others took the Intramural Railroad to many exciting points on the fairgrounds. Every day there was something new to explore, and every day there were thousands of new visitors to do the exploring.

Since the Chicago fair had attracted well over twenty million people, President Francis ultimately reported—with more than slight exaggeration—that twenty million had come to St. Louis. The number of paid visitors was actually closer to thirteen million, but there were about seven million employees, exhibitors, concessionaires, and children who came for free during the autumn. The visitors were as diverse as the attractions themselves. Walter H. Page noted: "You may make the acquaintance of a farmer and his family from Kansas, a teacher (of either sex) from Massachusetts, a cotton-planter from Georgia, a cattle-raiser from Texas—all within an hour or two, if you have even the slightest knack of making yourself interesting."[1]

One of the most curious visitors of all was a photographer named Jessie Tarbox Beals. With her husband, Alfred, she had moved to St. Louis soon before Opening Day in hopes of finding a job taking pictures of the fair for national newspapers. Though she found the competition among photographers fierce, Beals refused to give up. She managed to capture some exclusive shots of the South American "Patagonian Giants," who had just arrived at the fairgrounds and did not like having their pictures taken. When fair officials saw the high quality of these photographs, they gave Beals a full permit to photograph the fair; she was the first woman to receive one. For the rest of the fair, Beals could often be found in the company of President Francis, or lugging her heavy equipment to nearly every important event of the day. She even took pictures from nine hundred feet above the fairgrounds, aboard a hot-air balloon. President Francis was so amazed by her energy and enthusiasm that he awarded Beals a gold medal for her excellent contribution to the fair's success.

As Beals soon discovered, the fair had a strong international flavor because of the great numbers of people who had come from Europe,

Asia, Africa, the Americas, and Australia. However, not everyone in this diverse crowd was treated with equal respect. A century ago many white Americans held deep prejudices against people of color.

Eskimo girl Nancy Columbia smiles with one of her sled dogs. Nancy lived at the fair with her family, but it was not her first world's fair. She had been born in Chicago in 1893, when her parents had participated in the World's Columbian Exposition.

Unfortunately, racism and unequal treatment were widespread in cities, neighborhoods, schools, and businesses across the country. At the fair, too, mistreatment became all too common.

Although blacks made up nearly 10 percent of the St. Louis population—and had been an important part of the city's history since its founding in 1764—they experienced much hostility and discrimination at the fair. President Francis and other fair organizers often excluded blacks from planning events or working on the grounds. Black construction workers in particular found it difficult to find steady employment, even though they valuably contributed to the building of the palaces and many other structures.

Black leaders in St. Louis had lobbied tirelessly for the organization of Negro Day, which would feature parades, concerts, military exhibitions, and other attractions showcasing the achievements of blacks. They barely convinced fair organizers to schedule the events for August 1. But racism at the fair continued to spark complaints—especially from the Eighth Illinois, an all-black army regiment of nine hundred men planning to march in the Negro Day Parade. The soldiers were not allowed to stay on the fairgrounds and were ordered to pitch their tents elsewhere. In response the regiment refused to take part in Negro Day, and soon black leaders from St. Louis and other cities decided to cancel the entire day's events as an act of protest. While celebrations like Colonial Dames Day, Machinery Day, and Automobile Day took place, Negro Day never did.

Racism's ugly presence at the fair even affected Scott Joplin, the great ragtime composer and pianist. Having lived in Missouri for most of his life, Joplin was excited that the World's Fair had come to St. Louis. He even wrote "The Cascades" in honor of the fair's elegant waterfall. But though Joplin was one of the most famous musicians in the world, he was not allowed to perform in the Main Picture, where countless bands entertained. After much objection, he finally played on the Pike, along with many other black music and theater groups.

The Eighth Illinois regiment and Scott Joplin were not alone in receiving unfair treatment because of their race. During the summer of 1904, newspapers reported numerous other cases of discrimination—sometimes by fairgoers, and sometimes by employees and exhibitors. By the time autumn arrived, frustrated black leaders in St. Louis encouraged blacks to boycott the fair, and many were so disgusted with the racism they encountered that they stopped coming altogether.

While blacks were not the only minority group treated with disrespect, at least they were free to boycott the fair if they wanted. Others were not able to protest. Several ethnic groups had been brought from their homelands to St. Louis—in some cases by force. Men, women, and children were put on display so that fairgoers could take a first-hand look at them and, in theory, learn about their cultures.

The largest of these "anthropological" exhibits came from the Philippines. Hundreds of exploited Filipinos lived on the fairgrounds in open huts and flimsy thatched cabins. Cramped and filthy, the housing offered almost no privacy. The Filipinos were forced by fair managers to sit quietly while crowds of curious visitors gawked at them; they were also told to sing, dance, and perform other activities against their will. Instead of learning about the Filipinos and gaining respect for this culture, most fairgoers concluded they were a primitive race of inferior beings.

Native Americans, South Americans, and Africans brought to the fair were also forced to stay in makeshift living quarters. The exhibitors not only tried to show the "primitive" states of their cultures but also how "civilized" they could become with American influence and education. In

Young archers take aim in the Philippine Exhibit.

An entire community of Philippine Igorots came to St. Louis in 1904. Here, an Igorot demonstrates his skills.

"model" schools, similar to those in the Palace of Education and Social Economy, American teachers instructed foreign children in English without regard to their native languages and traditions. Sadly, most fairgoers did not question whether this "education" was right or wrong.

A number of these ethnic groups lived on the fairgrounds during the entire seven months of the fair. When the weather grew cold, they tried to keep warm in their temporary homes and struggled to preserve their own ways of life as much as possible. Undernourished, freezing, and often homesick, a few of these people even died during the fair, never to return to their homelands again.

Some people were disturbed by the exploitation of ethnic groups, including a magazine reporter named Laura Ingalls Wilder. Long before the Little House on the Prairie books made her a well-known children's author, she traveled from her home in southern Missouri to write about the fair. Wilder enjoyed the palaces, foreign buildings, and the Pike, but she was appalled by the mistreatment of many of the foreign and Native American people. She reportedly even tried to

African Pygmies dance in a performance in the Main Picture.

stop exhibitors from forcing them on display. One day, a young man from Africa was being exploited during a typically cruel stage show. Wilder stood up in the middle of the audience and demanded that the show stop immediately. The crowd fell silent, realizing that they had been laughing at the misfortune of another human being. But while Wilder fought injustice at the fair, she did not succeed in putting an end to such exhibitions.

Especially toward the end of the fair, when children under twelve received free admission, the Model Playground was one of the most diverse areas of the fair.

The exploitation of ethnic groups at the fair was similar to the kinds of discrimination that took place at most world's fairs around this time. Some people noticed it more than others. Many fairgoers would recall the countless faces of the fair with nothing but happiness. Others, however, could not help but feel the scars of mistreatment and injustice for many years afterward. Racism would be increasingly recognized as a destructive force in twentieth-century America. It was one more aspect of modern culture that was, unfortunately, quite well represented at the fair.

CHAPTER 9

☞ Special Events ☜

THE FAIR'S FESTIVE ATMOSPHERE CONTINUED through the late summer, with millions of fairgoers enjoying the palaces and foreign buildings, the Pike and the Ferris wheel. But President Francis wanted to make sure everyone kept coming back for more. So during the last several months of the fair, he scheduled as many special events as possible—from brand-new exhibits to parades and dramatic pageants. These surprises lured visitors to Forest Park for even more fun and adventure.

President Francis planned a number of popular exhibits with historical themes. He followed up on the fair's theme with several celebrations devoted to the Louisiana Purchase and the westward expansion of the United States. People were also interested in events commemorating the Civil War, fought only forty years earlier, and enjoyed watching Union and Confederate veterans march together in military parades. One popular exhibit displayed weapons and uniforms from the Battle of

◄ Splash! *The climactic scene from the Boer War featured horse and rider escaping from pursuing enemies by jumping into a deep pool of water.*

Gettysburg, along with large models and maps of the battlefield. Hundreds of performers participated in daily reenactments, dramatizing in a short performance the bloody, three-day battle from 1863. A tall, bearded speaker who looked just like Abraham Lincoln concluded the performance by delivering the famous Gettysburg Address, reminding everyone of the sacrifices made by those who fought in the Civil War.

Another military attraction pitted British and Boer (South African) forces against each other in a reenactment of a battle from the Three Years War of 1899–1902, also known as the Boer War. The climax featured a chase scene in which a rider portraying legendary Boer general Christiaan De Wet escaped the British on horseback. He would gallop at full speed before jumping his horse off an incredible thirty-foot cliff into a pool of water. Horse and rider performed this battle scene several times daily, so over the course of seven months this odd couple may have taken the plunge more than five hundred times! This attraction was noteworthy also for the way it distorted history. In the actual war British soldiers had massacred defenseless South African women and children, but when they performed at the fair, the British demanded that such events be omitted. They wanted spectators to see their soldiers only as heroic, honorable men, even if it meant misrepresenting the facts of history.

American forefathers and heroes of the Revolutionary War also received much attention. George Washington was honored in an exhibit sponsored by his home state of Virginia. Thomas Jefferson was remembered not just for the Louisiana Purchase but also for his role in writing the Declaration of Independence. Edward V. P. Schneiderhahn visited this exhibit on a rainy July 4 and described his experience: "Read the Declaration of Independence. It always sends a thrill through you to read the opening sentence 'When in the course of human events. . . .'"[1]

Police officers from Philadelphia accompanied the Liberty Bell to St. Louis and through the fairgrounds. This famous bell visited a number of expositions between 1885 and 1915, increasing its popularity across the country.

Even the Liberty Bell came to the fair that summer—after seventy-five thousand St. Louis school children had signed a petition requesting its visit. On June 8 the cracked bell arrived on a flat wagon pulled by a team of horses and surrounded by policemen from Philadelphia. Crowds lined the edges of the Plaza of St. Louis, hoping to get a glimpse of this famous artifact. Mayor Rolla Wells pronounced the occasion Liberty Bell Day and called off school in the city so that children could come to the fair. After the parade the Liberty Bell was placed temporarily in the Pennsylvania State Building for thousands more to see.

Fairgoers also crammed into the Plaza of St. Louis to watch pageants. These were short plays dramatizing historical events, such as the signing of the Declaration of Independence or the emancipation of American slaves. A single pageant often included hundreds of actors performing a few simple scenes—and perhaps a song or two—often followed by a band concert or military drill. The audience had the chance to imagine what it might have been like to witness these landmark events in person.

SPECIAL DAYS

To encourage a constant flow of visitors from all over the country, President Francis organized special days for every state. People from these states poured into the fairgrounds to celebrate with parades and cultural attractions. Thirty-two American cities also had their own special days. Thousands of visitors flocked to St. Louis for Chicago Day,

The biggest day of the fair: St. Louis Day, September 15. The crowds crammed the fairgrounds for the day's festivities.

a friendly tribute to St. Louis's northern rival. However, St. Louis Day set the record for daily attendance by drawing 358,403 visitors on September 15. The Main Picture was filled all day long with parades, concerts, and merriment, while the Pike's celebration lasted until police forced everyone to go home late at night.

Individual days were also devoted to several countries, such as Ireland, Germany, and Scotland. While fewer people made a special trip from these distant lands, many Americans, especially recent immigrants from Europe, saw the days as opportunities to celebrate their diverse ethnic backgrounds. On November 5 a large contingent of Irish Americans converged on the fairgrounds for Ireland

Day, turning the fair into a sea of green, white, and orange flags and celebrating late into the evening.

Hundreds of smaller clubs and organizations, from Elks and Shriners to scientific, intellectual, and artistic societies, held conferences and meetings in St. Louis and then enjoyed the fair afterward. The fair also served as an important site for the advancement of higher learning, bringing together leading scholars from New York City, Vienna, Copenhagen, Stockholm, and many other places. President Francis had wanted the fair to show how knowledge and learning would serve as progressive forces in the twentieth century, so the presence of these scholarly congresses fit in well with the fair's larger purpose.

OLYMPIC GAMES

St. Louis was the first American city to host the Olympic Games, which took place for six days in late August and early September. Since the modern Olympics had only begun in 1896, the Games had not yet become as popular as they are today. Most of the competitors were not world-class athletes from around the world but enthusiastic American amateurs. They participated primarily in track-and-field competitions and swimming races held in the Life Savings Exhibit Lake. But there were also a few unusual events for them to try, such as a tug-of-war tournament, competitive croquet, and football games.

Only a few nations sent athletes to participate. Some were prevented from traveling there because of the ongoing Russo-Japanese War. More

The Olympics included a number of unusual events like tug-of-war, football, one-handed weight lifting, and the rope climb.

commonly, however, athletes decided not to come because they believed St. Louis was a Wild West town, full of cowboys and Indians, gunfights and war dances. But those who came to compete soon learned what St. Louis was really like; many of them enjoyed their visits so much that they decided to stay and live in the city for good. George Coleman Poage, a hurdler from Milwaukee, was one such athlete. After winning bronze medals in the two-hundred- and four-hundred-meter hurdle races, Poage settled down in St. Louis and became a successful businessman. He was the first black athlete ever to win a medal in the Olympic Games.

Because the Games were fairly new—and therefore disorganized—
many bizarre and amusing things happened. After a disagreement over
who won the fifty-meter race, two swimmers got into a brawl and just
agreed to race again. There was no such thing as instant replay in 1904,
of course. And American gymnast George Eyser ambled off with five
medals, including two golds, after competing with a wooden leg. He
had lost one leg after being run over by a train years earlier.

But it was the marathon that provided the funniest stories from the
Games. A Cuban postman named Felix Carvajal barely made it to the

George Coleman Poage, third from the right, finished the 400-meter hurdles in third place. This victory made him the first black athlete to win an Olympic medal.

starting line because he had gambled away all his money in New Orleans and had to hitchhike the rest of the way to St. Louis. He arrived just as the race was about to begin and had to run in his street clothes. Carvajal turned out to be a great runner—and may have had a chance to win the race—but he kept stopping along the course to eat fruit. First he stole some peaches from a race official; then, a few miles later, he sneaked into an orchard for a few green apples. Despite these pit stops, he still managed to finish fourth. A pair of Zulu tribesmen, Len Taunyane and Jan Mashiani, became the first African athletes to compete in the Olympics, even though they were supposed to be part of the Boer War Exhibit. Taunyane might have won, but a fierce dog chased him nearly a mile off course, and he finished in ninth place.

Fred Lorz from New York City was the first marathoner to enter the stadium, and thousands of spectators exploded with cheers when he arrived. After crossing the finish line, Lorz received the winner's trophy and posed for a photograph with Alice Roosevelt, the president's daughter. But soon everyone learned that Lorz had cheated by hitching a ride for about ten miles of the race! When confronted, Lorz just shrugged and said he had not meant to fool anybody but just wanted to enjoy the applause of the huge crowd. By the time the real winner, Thomas Hicks, arrived, many spectators had grown angry and left the scene. The exhausted Hicks, who had consumed a mixture of egg whites, brandy, and strychnine during the race to sustain his strength, collapsed on the track. Four doctors helped Hicks walk out of the stadium, and a while later the new Olympic champion fell asleep on a streetcar.

In addition to hosting the Olympics, organizers sponsored what they called Anthropology Days, in which members of the "uncivilized races" competed against one another in a series of strange contests. Unfortunately, many Filipinos, Native Americans, and other ethnic minorities were forced to compete in sports that they had never seen before. These events—including mud fighting, pole climbing, and rock throwing—were designed to make participants look as primitive as

As part of Anthropology Days, Native Americans took part in competitions, including this archery contest. However, they were also forced to take part in ridiculous activities such as greased-pole climbing and mud fighting.

possible. Several of these ethnic groups also took part in traditional events, demonstrating skill and dexterity and showing great pride in their physical abilities. A Native American archery competition in the late summer proved to be a popular event for both spectators and contestants, as several tribes tried to outdo one another with bow and arrow.

CHAPTER 10

Present's Day, Francis Day, and Farewell

A S THE WEATHER GREW COLDER, orange and red leaves began falling from trees. The fair's closing day, December 1, was drawing near. Fairgoers came more and more often, hurrying around the park to make sure they didn't miss anything. Among these busy visitors was Edward V. P. Schneiderhahn, who described the frustration in his diary. "Get too impatient now and must use will power to keep at one thing. A sort of nervous tension to try to do too many things at once. It is ridiculous but the pressure is there."[1]

PRESIDENT'S DAY

But President Francis had planned one last special day to mark the fair—a day for the president of the United States. Shortly after 9:00 A.M. on November 26, President Theodore Roosevelt emerged from

◄ *President Roosevelt (far left) watches a parade in his honor, while President Francis (standing behind banner) looks on.*

Roosevelt's energetic style fit right in with the spirit of the Pike.

his railroad car. With his wife, Edith, and daughter Alice (who had spent a lot of time at the fair on her own), he was greeted by a crowd of two hundred thousand people who had come for President's Day.

Known for his tremendous energy, President Roosevelt outran even his own security force in an amazing, one-day whirlwind tour of the entire fair. Along the Plaza of St. Louis he watched a military parade featuring more than two thousand soldiers. He also received works of art from several countries, including sculpture from Italy and a Chinese painting that was at least eight hundred years old. Perhaps the most unusual gift was a bolo knife from an old warrior at the Philippine Exhibit. He told President Roosevelt that he had killed three people in battle with the knife but had no use for it anymore. The president happily accepted the gift.

In the evening the Roosevelts watched colorful fireworks explode above the Cascades; when quiet returned to the skies, white lights illuminated the fairgrounds. Six hundred guests attended a banquet in President Roosevelt's honor at the Tyrolean Alps. "I count it, indeed, a privilege to have had a chance of visiting this marvelous Exposition," he exclaimed. "It is in very fact, the greatest Exposition of the kind that we have ever seen in recorded history."[2] The guests gave a huge ovation, bursting with pride at the president's praise for St. Louis and its World's Fair.

After the banquet, President Roosevelt wanted to see even more of the fairgrounds and took a short carriage ride through the Plateau of States. The next day President Roosevelt rested at the home of President Francis before leaving. As his train pulled away from St. Louis, a newspaper reporter asked President Roosevelt how he had liked his visit to the fair. He replied, "Why, my boy, I've had the time of my life!"[3]

FRANCIS DAY

During the final days of the fair, crowds of people followed President Francis around the grounds, shouting their thanks and support. Despite his exhaustion and relief, he maintained his busy pace. The last day of the fair was named Francis Day in his honor by the other fair organizers. Governor Alexander Monroe Dockery declared December 1 a state holiday for Missouri, and businesses and schools closed for the day.

Early that morning, enormous crowds gathered in every corner of Forest Park. It seemed as if the entire population of St. Louis had arrived for the most triumphant—and saddest—day of the fair. What had been a part of their lives for seven months would disappear after the stroke of midnight. Farewell celebrations began early on the Pike; by midday, fairgoers congregated to sing and enjoy the last of the grand street performances.

President Francis made several speeches, expressing his great pride in the fair and his sadness that it must come to an end. He toured the fairgrounds one last time, fighting back tears as he looked upon the majestic palaces. That evening he was honored at a banquet hosted by the other fair organizers, who thanked him for his leadership. They all realized how President Francis had changed the course of their city's history; he had wanted to host the greatest world's fair of all time in St. Louis—and he turned that dream into a reality.

Later in the evening, President Francis drove past huge, noisy crowds on the Pike, then joined even larger crowds on the Plaza of St. Louis. Everyone was dressed for the cold weather, in long winter coats and gloves, but the atmosphere was warm with excitement. The people cheered President Francis as he found his place near the Louisiana Monument, where he had stood on Opening Day. The illumination of so many thousands of white lights on the Main Picture presented one last beautiful image. "I am about to perform a heart-rending duty," President Francis announced sadly, gazing over the Grand Basin

The lovely lights of Festival Hall would live on in the memories of all those who had visited St. Louis in 1904.

at the Cascades and the palaces.[4] At the stroke of midnight, he flipped the switch that turned off the fair's spectacular lights for one last time, and the scene slowly faded to darkness. At that moment one last display of fireworks exploded overhead. On one of the palaces, a large portrait of President Francis glowed in white light next to the words *Farewell* and *Good Night*. The Louisiana Purchase Exposition—the magnificent St. Louis World's Fair of 1904—was over. The last glow eventually faded, but the memory of the fair would live on within all those who had been a part of it.

Remembering the Fair

AFTER THE FAIR THE CITY OF ST. LOUIS would see a great deal of change. Everyone returned to the daily lives they had known before, the lives that had been so pleasantly interrupted for seven months in 1904. The rumbling streetcars no longer brought so many wide-eyed, diverse visitors to the park. Owners of private homes and rooming houses said good-bye to their guests from around the world. President Francis returned most of his energy to his business career and later returned to politics, serving as the American ambassador to Russia from 1916 to 1918. With his wife and six grown sons, he remained firmly rooted in St. Louis no matter where his travels took him. In 1927 Francis died at the age of seventy-six.

125

Forest Park began to look like its old self again, although it would take several years for the transformation to occur. Many of its largest trees were gone, and it would take decades before new ones grew to

A poster advertises the 1944 movie Meet Me in St. Louis, *just like posters and billboards had advertised the fair itself forty years earlier.*

Visitors locked away fun memories of St. Louis.

replace them. Because of the sheer expense of demolition, some palaces and other large buildings were left standing for months, even years. A number of Pike concessionaires, motivated more by greed than affection for St. Louis, left town without dismantling their buildings. Eventually curious visitors—including many who had watched the construction in the park with great interest—paid twenty-five cents to watch the buildings fall. Often people were invited to haul away whatever remains they could salvage. In other cases the materials were sold to companies that would reuse them. A businessman named John D. Wanamaker purchased Festival Hall's booming pipe organ and transported it by train to his department store in Philadelphia, where shoppers can still hear its deep sound a century later.

A few of the state and national buildings enjoyed a second life after the world's fair. Maine's log cabin was purchased by a hunting club, which rebuilt it as their lodge in central Missouri. Smaller buildings from states including Utah, Nevada, and New Hampshire were bought and moved to different parts of the St. Louis area, where they still stand as private homes. Adolphus Busch purchased the Belgium national building and converted it into a bottle factory for his sprawling Anheuser-Busch brewery just south of downtown St. Louis.

Some people wanted the Pike to remain a permanent fixture on the north border of the park. Adolphus Busch wanted to build a new theater and beer garden where the Tyrolean Alps had stood; others wanted to build a large stadium and a beach for five thousand people. In the end, however, Washington University professors objected; they worried that students might ignore their schoolwork if the Pike were so close to campus. Today a strip of stately mansions occupies the Pike's former home, quietly keeping the secrets of a noisy, action-packed seven months in 1904.

The only surviving palace was the Palace of Fine Arts, which soon began its new life as the St. Louis Art Museum. A majestic statue of St. Louis now stands in place of Festival Hall, as if recalling the scene of the bustling crowds and the magnificent palaces below on the Main Picture. The Plateau of States gave way to the St. Louis Zoo; its large, domed birdcage is one of the only architectural remnants of the fair. In 1913 the Jefferson Memorial was built on the site of the fair's main entrance. The first national monument dedicated to the president who had secured the Louisiana Territory, this large building housed the

For fond recollections at every meal:
a Ferris wheel dinner plate

Let us go, then, you and I . . . to the fair! Sixteen-year-old Tom Eliot seems to have loved the fair—forty-nine of fifty admisssion tickets in his ticket book were used. The budding poet, later known as T. S. Eliot, grew up on the eastern edge of Forest Park.

collections of the Missouri Historical Society and the Louisiana Purchase Exposition Company. Today it is known simply as the Missouri History Museum and includes a large addition that was opened in 2000. Where the Missouri State Building had stood before its devastating fire, a lovely open-air pavilion now stands as a memorial to the fair. In time golf courses, tennis courts, and one of the largest outdoor theaters in the United States would be built on the old fairgrounds. Today Forest Park continues to be a treasure in St. Louis, where many people come to relax, to exercise, and to go sledding down Art Hill (as the site of the Cascades has become known) each snowy winter.

Fairgoers preserved collections of memorabilia to remind them of the fair. Programs, postcards, photographs, ticket stubs, beer mugs, and belt buckles became tangible pieces of the fair's history. Many children, grandchildren, and even great-grandchildren of fairgoers continue to collect memorabilia today. In the last several decades, archaeologists have conducted digs in Forest Park, seeking to unearth more artifacts from the fair that might have been buried accidentally. These items often provide a feeling of connection to the fair—a sense of what it might have really been like to explore the palaces, relax near the Cascades, or ride the Ferris wheel on a clear summer day in 1904.

Many stories about visits to the fair were published over the next few years. Often these were amusing tales about the wild adventures of small-town people from around the United States. In 1944 a vibrant movie called *Meet Me in St. Louis* was produced, based on the short stories of a St. Louis native named Sally Benson. Benson's family had moved to New York when she was still a small child, and she never got to visit the fair; in her stories, however, she imagined how nice it would have been to stay in St. Louis. *Meet Me in St. Louis* introduced the world's fair to a whole new generation of Americans, many of whom had never even heard of it. The

Each spoon in this collection features a different palace, serving up memories of the fair.

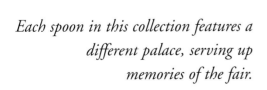

129

title song had been a popular tune back in 1904. Its verses told funny stories about different people and animals who wanted to come to the fair. When the movie came out, the chorus became popular again.

As the years passed, great world's fairs became rarer and rarer. After World War I events such as the Louisiana Purchase Exposition would become virtually extinct. All the fair's inventions and glimpses into the future—telegraphs and telephones, the popularization of automobile and airplane travel—had the strange effect of making the world feel like a smaller place. The western United States was no longer viewed

Thousands of stereograph cards like this one were produced and sold at the fair, keeping images of St. Louis alive long after 1904. The double image produced a 3-D effect when seen through a contraption called a stereo viewer.

as an open frontier with limitless resources, but simply another developed region of the country. The far corners of the world also seemed less mysterious, less exotic, and people felt less need to bring the whole world to one place anymore. While there would be other world's fairs and expositions, none would ever match the grandeur, imaginativeness, or sheer sprawling size of the 1904 St. Louis World's Fair.

What can we see, then, as we gaze back at this strange and wondrous fair? We see what we used to be like, and how we have changed since then. Looking back is like that first Ferris wheel ride: frightening, exhilarating, adventurous, fun, and promising—always promising. Perhaps, like that wonderful first flight into the clear blue sky, looking back will even help us to see, just a little, where we might be headed in the future—and how much adventure there will be in getting there, too.

Calendar of Events

In addition to major events such as the Olympic Games, St. Louis Day, and President's Day, all sorts of special days were planned at the fair. Here are some of the most significant dates:

April 30, 1903	Dedication Day
April 30, 1904	Opening Day
June 7	Alabama Day
June 8	Liberty Bell parade
June 17	Iowa Day
July 4	Independence Day
August 13	Philippine Day
August 20	Pennsylvania Day
August 21–26	Missouri Week
August 29–September 3	Olympic Games
September 5	Oklahoma Day
September 9	California Day
September 12	Texas Day
September 14	Louisiana Day
September 15	St. Louis Day
September 17	Massachusetts Day
September 22	Virginia Day
October 6	New Jersey Day
October 8	Maine Day
October 18	Alaska Day
November 5	Ireland Day
November 26	President's Day
December 1	Francis Day

World's Fairs & Expositions

Starting in 1851 with London's exposition, only a few world's fairs reached the truly magnificent dimensions of St. Louis's in 1904. Paris, London's rival across the English Channel, held fairs in 1855, 1867, 1878, 1889, and 1900 (and another in 1937), but only its 1900 exposition ranks with the largest of its time. Here are some of the most significant world's fairs:

1851	London, England	Great Exhibition of the Works of Industry of All Nations
1873	Vienna, Austria	Weltausstellung 1873
1876	Philadelphia	Centennial Exposition
1893	Chicago	World's Columbian Exposition
1895	Atlanta	Cotton States International Exposition
1900	Paris	Exposition Universelle Internationale
1901	Buffalo	Pan-American Exposition
1904	St. Louis	Louisiana Purchase Exposition
1910	Brussels, Belgium	Exposition Universelle et Internationale
1915	San Francisco	Panama Pacific International Exposition
1939	New York	New York World's Fair
1962	Seattle	Century 21 Exposition
1964–5	New York	New York World's Fair

Endnotes

CHAPTER 2: PREPARING FOR THE WORLD

1. Martha Clevenger, ed., *Indescribably Grand: Diaries and Letters from the 1904 World's Fair* (St. Louis: Missouri Historical Society Press, 1996), p. 130.

2. Theodore Roosevelt, "Address at the Dedication Ceremonies of the Louisiana Purchase Exposition" (http://www.boondocksnet.com/oxpos/wfe_tr030430.html).

CHAPTER 3: OPENING DAY AT THE MAIN PICTURE

1. David R. Francis, *The Universal Exposition of 1904* (St. Louis: Louisiana Purchase Exposition Company, 1913), p. 174.

2. Clevenger, p. 146.

CHAPTER 4: INSIDE THE PALACES

1. Lillian Brandt, "Department of Social Economy at St. Louis" (http://www.boondocksnet.com/oxpos/wfe_louisiana_cc040702.html).

2. *Ibid.*

3. Clevenger, p. 49.

4. *Ibid.*, p. 98.

5. *Ibid.*, p. 80.

6. "How to See the Fair" (http://www.boondocksnet.com/oxpos/wfe_how_to_see.html).

CHAPTER 5: WIDE WORLD OF ARCHITECTURE

1. Walter H. Page, "The People as an Exhibit" (http://www.boondocksnet.com/oxpos/wfe_1904_people.html).

Chapter 6: Illusions on the Pike

1. Clevenger, p. 142.
2. *Ibid.*, p. 144.
3. *Ibid.*, p. 88.

Chapter 7: The Great Wheel

1. *Ibid.*, p. 84.
2. Bert Minkin, *Legacies of the St. Louis World's Fair* (St. Louis: Virginia Publishing, 1998), p. 51.
3. John Wayne Tucker, "The Remains of a Dream" (http://walden.mo.net/~tucker/wfair5.html).
4. Clevenger, p. 140.

Chapter 8: Faces of the Fair

1. Page.

Chapter 9: Special Events

1. Clevenger, p. 43.

Chapter 10: President's Day, Francis Day, and Farewell

1. *Ibid.*, p. 49.
2. Minkin, p. 93.
3. *Ibid.*, p. 94.
4. Francis, p. 307.

Selected Bibliography

Brandt, Lillian. "Department of Social Economy at St. Louis." *Charities* 12 (July 2, 1904).

Clevenger, Martha, ed. *Indescribably Grand: Diaries and Letters from the 1904 World's Fair.* St. Louis: Missouri Historical Society Press, 1996.

Fox, Timothy J., and Duane R. Sneddeker. *From the Palaces to the Pike: Visions of the 1904 World's Fair.* St. Louis: Missouri Historical Society Press, 1997.

"How to See the Fair." *The World's Work* 8 (August 1904).

Minkin, Bert. *Legacies of the St. Louis World's Fair.* St. Louis: Virginia Publishing, 1998.

Page, Walter H. "The People as an Exhibit." *The World's Work* 8 (August 1904).

Roosevelt, Theodore. *Addresses and Presidential Messages of Theodore Roosevelt, 1902–1904.* New York: G. P. Putnam's Sons, 1904.

☜ Suggested Reading ☞

If you'd like to read more about the Louisiana Purchase Exposition, St. Louis history, and other world's fairs, the following list includes fiction and nonfiction titles for both young readers and adults. For more background on the fair (and a wealth of great photographs and journals), see Timothy J. Fox and Duane R. Sneddeker's wonderful *From the Palaces to the Pike* and Martha Clevenger's *Indescribably Grand*. The best single book on St. Louis history is James Neal Primm's *Lion of the Valley*. Robert W. Rydell is one of a number of scholars who have studied and written about world's fairs in broad historical and political contexts. Marietta Holley, Herb Lewis, and C. M. Stevens all wrote humorous fiction about the fair in the early twentieth century. Richard Peck and Eleanora Tate have recently written children's fiction set against the backdrop of world's fairs. And of course, Sally Benson's collection *Meet Me in St. Louis* includes the short stories, originally published in *The New Yorker*, on which the 1944 movie was based.

(*) denotes books of particular interest to young readers.

NONFICTION

*Alter, Judy. *Meet Me at the Fair: Country, State, and World's Fairs and Expositions.* New York: Franklin Watts, 1997.

Birk, Dorothy Daniels. *The World Came to St. Louis: A Visit to the 1904 World's Fair.* St. Louis: Bethany Press, 1979.

Clevenger, Martha, ed. *Indescribably Grand: Diaries and Letters from the 1904 World's Fair.* St. Louis: Missouri Historical Society Press, 1996.

Fox, Timothy J., and Duane R. Sneddeker. *From the Palaces to the Pike: Visions of the 1904 World's Fair.* St. Louis: Missouri Historical Society Press, 1997.

*Hilton, Suzanne. *Here Today and Gone Tomorrow: The Story of World's Fairs and Expositions.* Philadelphia: Westminster Press, 1978.

Primm, James Neal. *Lion of the Valley: St. Louis, Missouri, 1764–1980.* St. Louis: Missouri Historical Society Press, 1998.

Rydell, Robert W. *All the World's a Fair: Visions of Empire at American International Expositions, 1876–1916.* Chicago: University of Chicago Press, 1984.

Rydell, Robert W., John E. Findling, and Kimberly D. Pelle. *Fair America: World's Fairs in the United States.* Washington: Smithsonian Institution Press, 2000.

FICTION

Benson, Sally. *Meet Me in St. Louis.* New York: Random House, 1942.

Holley, Marietta. *Samantha at the St. Louis Exposition, by Josiah Allen's Wife.* New York: G. W. Dillingham, 1904.

Lewis, Herb. *Eb Peechcrap and Wife at the Fair: Being the Experience of Residents of 'Possum Ridge, Arkansaw in St. Louis.* New York: Neale, 1906.

*Peck, Richard. "The Electric Summer." *Time Capsule: Short Stories About Teenagers Throughout the Twentieth Century.* ed. Donald R. Gallo. New York: Random House, 1999.

*———. *Fair Weather.* New York: Penguin, 2001.

Stevens, C. M. *Uncle Jeremiah and His Neighbors at the St. Louis Exposition.* Chicago: Thompson and Thomas, 1904.

*Tate, Eleanora. *The Minstrel's Melody* (An American Girl History Mysteries, 11). Middleton, Wisc.: Pleasant Company Publications, 2001.

Wolfe, Thomas. *The Lost Boy: A Novella.* Chapel Hill: University of North Carolina Press, 1992.

☞ Index ☜

References to illustrations are in *italics*.

✒ Acknowledgments ✒

This book would not exist without the extraordinary support of the Missouri Historical Society, whose library and research center across the street from the Ferris wheel site in Forest Park became a warm, comfortable home to me. Thanks are due to the entire MHS staff, and especially to Ellen Thomasson for her expertise with photographs and her encyclopedic knowledge of fair history. Amanda Claunch provided helpful assistance. The library staffs at Washington University, St. Louis University, St. Louis Public Library, St. Louis County Library, and the Library of Congress also offered invaluable support.

Individuals in St. Louis and elsewhere who deserve mention for contributing to the project in various ways, and for merely putting up with me, include Lois Adams, John and Diane Anderson, David "Longhair" Brandt, Kathy Brewer, Ethan Campbell, Yvonne Condon, Linda Dover, Kat Gasparich, Dabney Gray, Kirkley Greenwell, Susan Hirschman, Fred Hobson, Evan Karachalios, Larry and Jill Levy, Willa Lowe, Elizabeth McHenry, Esme Montgomery, Peggy Moser, Lara Narcisi, Joseph Pins, Colleen "C-Note" Reisenbichler, Michael Schwartz, Dave Snead and Sandy Lynn, Anne Stevens, Max Storm, Adam Tate, Barbara Trueson, Mary Ann "Ud" Virant, Denise Wilch, Drew Worseck, and Jim Zwick.

Two families were most directly involved. The first is my own: my parents, Bob and Nancy Jackson; my brothers, John and George; my sisters, Paula and Katie; and their children, my intended readers, Maya, Kathleen, John, Liam, and Elizabeth. To Cori Jane Jackson, my beloved Westie pup of seventeen years, goes a note of special thanks for steadfast loyalty: she was present, usually curled up near my feet, at every stage of the book's development—my first, and most forgiving, audience. The O'Brien clan was also key to my efforts: Mike, Bonnie, Dobs, Beth, Isabel, Eobs, Tim, Jenny, Becca, and Rosie. They fed me a good deal, often housed me, and generally provided a haven, in ways indescribable in words, comparable to that of my own family.

At HarperCollins, three individuals require special mention. The first is Barbara Lalicki, who, crucially and perhaps a bit inexplicably, trusted me to write. The second is Stephanie Bart-Horvath, a talented and enthusiastic designer. Finally, Rachel Orr, to whom this book is dedicated: an editor of relentless faith, discriminating eye, subtle palate, and coarse humor. To say that she believed in the book would be a prize understatement. She was, always in the best sense, my collaborator; and in truth, this book belongs to her.